VISITATION

To Cindy
God Bless
Art & Carolyn Perkins
perkusart44@gmail.com
360-832-6099

Visitation

An Intensely Personal Narrative

Art Perkins

To order additional copies of this book, contact:
Xlibris
1-888-795-4274
www.Xlibris.com
Orders@Xlibris.com
774878

Contents

PART ONE

THE EVENT

CHAPTER ONE

Odd Visions

I have recurring visions, more frequent now that I'm elderly. They remain ill-formed, but with each vision I seem to get a slightly deeper glimpse into what took place during the event that had such a profound impact on my life.

At first I didn't perceive any impact at all. I had thought of the event itself as strange, being an odd confirmation of an entire genre of stories recounting a multitude of like experiences. But I had no inkling that I would be personally affected, and in a way that would change my life.

The event itself, surrealistic as it was, quickly got pushed into the background amid more immediate matters at hand that demanded my time and focus. After a few months had passed, the event drifted away from conscious thought even to the extent that it didn't inhabit odd dreams or the like. Awake, or asleep, thoughts connected with the topic simply didn't come up. Or so I had supposed.

Nevertheless, something far outside the limit of my notion of reality was lurking somewhere in the subconscious region of my mind. Then, six months after the event, this new thing reached the surface of my mind and thrust upon me an uncontrollable urge to pick up a Bible and read the text within.

That urge itself represented the strangest event of all because I was an unbeliever. Everyone in my family was an agnostic. My parents and grandparents on my father's side, being self-proclaimed intellectuals, considered religion to be beneath an understanding of the world about them. Without giving the issue much thought, they simply knew that religious belief was inappropriate for their intellectual class. Having been brought up in that manner, we all were smugly content in the conviction that an objective God was nonexistent, nothing more than an invention of primitive, gullible, naïve, and exploitable humans. Only *untermenschen*, malcontents and emotional cripples believed the pap fed to them by priests and ministers in their bright robes and other elegant symbols of self-proclaimed authority. That lesser sort was incapable of adapting to the demands of modern society and was best left alone to suffer apart.

I should qualify the word "conviction" here. Conviction implies a focused attitude, which we didn't have. The subject of God rarely came up, and when it did we were too indifferent to care one way or another.

Nudging my agnosticism toward full-blown atheism was a sharply discouraging experience I had at one time with the Bible. Having forgotten to bring a book along for entertainment while on a business trip, I found myself in a hotel room without any reading material. Not wishing to get up and go looking for a bookstore, I looked in a drawer on the nightstand next to my bed and, sure enough, found a Gideon Bible. Turning to a random page, I came across Matthew 25 (I remember that part very well) and began to read. I barely understood a word of the passage and in frustration closed the Bible abruptly and put it back in the drawer. Reluctantly, I left my room and tramped outside the hotel in search of the nearest store that might carry some reading material more in line with my tastes. That one experience, as far as I was concerned, would be the last to involve a Bible.

I was very wrong. That wouldn't be the last time I'd pick up a Bible with the intent of reading it. Not by a long shot, for which I fervently thank our gracious God. My unquenchable desire to read the Bible had occurred about six months after the event of which I write. I didn't understand all of what I was reading in Scripture this time around, but I was amazed at the amount that I did. A year of nightly reading got me through the Bible from cover to cover. It was an emotion-charged experience, bringing me to laughter at times and to tears at others. Through His Word I came to know God to the point that I willingly asked Jesus into my heart and soul. My growth afterward as a Christian had its ups and downs, but He never forsook me, nor I Him. I'm exceedingly grateful for that.

Seven more years passed before I connected the event of which I write with the Christianity that it initiated. I was talking with another person at the time, giving him what details I could remember of the event itself, when another memory of a question that had persistently hounded me kept stubbornly intruding. Over that seven-year hiatus I had been laboring to find an answer to the pressing, even disturbing, question as to why I possessed an understanding of the Bible of a depth that astonished me, particularly for my background as a long-time unbeliever.

From where would that understanding come to an agnostic who couldn't understand one simple passage a few short years earlier? I certainly couldn't recollect having been visited by God or one of His angelic representatives. I questioned the source of not only my understanding, but my enthusiasm, which had taken my family by such complete surprise that they were coming close to demanding that I visit a competent psychiatrist, the alternative being that they would take some as-yet unspecified action on my behalf.

But then, in one heart-stopping instant as I talked with my friend, I suddenly realized that a visitation of that sort could have come from the very event that we had been discussing. Moreover, nothing else had taken place in my past that could have accounted for the knowledge of God that I now possessed. The connection was made. Full confirmation of the link came later, when I began to have flashbacks to a very informative conversation, one in which I was told of things in my future both joyfully positive and, most sadly, severely negative that were in my future. They came to pass, all of them. I remember the feeling of desperate yearning that the foretold events would be in my past, permitting me to emerge into the glorious light thereafter that had been promised.

Chapter Two

Jesus' Supernatural Features

Jesus set the bar on nobility enormously high. Ever since my Drill Instructor informed us feckless recruits that we'd be paying for his father's death on the Tarawa battlefield, I've had an image of the noble spirit of those Marines who waded into continuous machine gun fire, having a pretty good idea of what the odds were against their survival. But Jesus outdid them. What it must have taken Jesus – God – to step down into our world, knowing to the most minute detail the suffering He'd have to endure as he gave His life for the sake of His love toward us must have been the most selflessly noble act in the history of the universe. I suppose that Christians get that. Actually, they must, or they wouldn't be Christians.

On the other hand, there have been a lot of self-styled Christians in this world, now and into the distant past, who have understood very little of the basics of the Judeo-Christian God and even less of the Bible, His Word to mankind, so I'm not too sure of even that.

But there's one thing I'm pretty certain of. I'd be willing to bet that maybe only one person out of a hundred – or perhaps even a thousand or more – has read John 20 and wondered about the odd nature of the spiritual domain.

Perhaps, being clued in to something special about that chapter by my brief commentary above, the reader will perceive its odd features:

> *"Then the same day at evening, being the first day of the week, when the doors were shut where the disciples were assembled for fear of the Jews, came [the resurrected] Jesus and stood in the midst, and saith unto them, Peace be unto you. . . And, after eight days, again*

his disciples were inside, and Thomas with them; then came Jesus, the doors being shut, and stood in the midst, and said, Peace be unto you. Then saith he to Thomas, Reach here thy finger, and behold my hands; and reach here thy hand, and thrust it into my side; and be not faithless, but believing. And Thomas answered, and said unto him, My Lord, and my God."

Really? Standing in their midst, the doors being shut? Here, the inescapable conclusion is that Jesus arrives through solid walls and appears solid enough Himself that Thomas has to thrust his hand into Him to believe Him. Obviously, the risen Jesus possesses features and capabilities beyond those associated with the material domain inhabited by us mortals. In fact, when we label our domain as "material", we wrongly imply by that that the spiritual domain is not. The passage noted above should make it clear that the spiritual domain is entirely capable of manifesting material features.

Material enough, according to Genesis 6, for spiritual entities to mate with humans and produce offspring capable of dominating the material domain.

There's more. In Luke 4:28-30, the passage begins with an affirmation of Jesus' solidity and ends with an affirmation of Jesus' capability either to shape-shift or to become invisible, even before His death and resurrection:

"And all they in the synagogue, when they heard these things, were filled with wrath. And rose up, and thrust him out of the city, and led him unto the brow of the hill on which their city was built, that they might cast him down headlong. But he, passing through the midst of them, went his way."

Comparing John 13:36-38 with John 18:17 and 25-27, Jesus knew –intimately- of things to come. In the spiritual domain, time is understood so differently that it furnishes knowledge of the future within the material domain:

"Simon Peter said unto him, Lord, where goest thou? Jesus answered him, Where I go, thou canst not follow me now; but thou shalt follow me afterwards. Peter said unto him, Lord, why cannot I follow thee now? I will lay down my life for thy sake. Jesus answered him, Wilt thou lay down thy life for my sake? Verily, verily, I say unto thee, The cock shall not crow, till thou hast denied me thrice."

> *"Then saith the maid that kept the door unto Peter, Art not thou also one of this man's disciples? He saith, I am not. . . And Simon Peter stood and warmed himself. They said, therefore, unto him, Art not thou also one of his disciples? He denied it, and said, I am not. One of the servants of the high priest, being his kinsman whose ear Peter cut off, saith, Did not I see thee in the garden with him? Peter then denied again; and immediately the cock crowed."*

Moreover, according to John 18:4-6 and 19:11, God and perhaps others within the spiritual domain are capable of influencing matters in the material domain, including the capability of granting and withholding material power:

> *"Jesus, therefore, knowing all things that should come upon him, went forth, and said unto them, Whom seek ye? They answered him, Jesus of Nazareth. Jesus saith unto them, I am. And Judas also, who betrayed him, stood with them. As soon, then, as he had said unto them, I am, they went backward, and fell to the ground."*

> *"Jesus answered, Thou [Pilate] couldest have no power at all against me, except it were given thee from above; therefore, he that delivered me unto thee hath the greater sin."*

The power to foretell the future has been granted by God to selected individuals within the material domain, permitting us to become aware not only of the greater world beyond ours but also of the vast difference between the spiritual and material worlds. Perhaps the most stark and certainly the most well-documented example of what we would consider the supernatural ability to know the future is given in the comparison of Zechariah 9:9, Daniel 9:25 and Nehemiah 1:11-2:1-8 with Matthew 21:1-9:

> *'And when they drew near unto Jerusalem, and were come to Bethphage, unto the Mount of Olives, then sent Jesus two disciples, Saying unto them, Go into the village opposite you, and straightway ye shall find an ass tied, and a colt with her; loose them, and bring them unto me. And if any man say anything unto you, ye shall say, The Lord hath need of them; and straightway he will send them. All this was done, that it might be fulfilled which was spoken by the prophet, saying, Tell ye the daughter of Zion, Behold, thy King cometh unto thee, meek, and sitting upon an ass, and a colt, the foal*

of an ass. And the disciples went, and did as Jesus commanded them, and brought the ass, and the colt, and put on them their clothes, and they set him thereon. And a very great multitude spread their garments in the way; others cut down branches from the trees, and spread them in the way. And the multitudes that went before, and that followed, cried, saying, Hosanna to the Son of David! Blessed is he that cometh in the name of the Lord! Hosanna in the Highest!"

"Rejoice greatly, daughter of Zion; shout, O daughter of Jerusalem; behold, thy King cometh unto thee; he is just, and having salvation; lowly, and riding upon an ass, and upon a colt, the foal of an ass. . . Know, therefore, and understand, that from the going forth of the commandment to restore and to build Jerusalem unto the Messiah, the Prince, shall be seven weeks, and threescore and two weeks; the street shall be built again, and the wall, even in troublous times. . . O Lord, I beseech thee, let now thine ear be attentive to the prayer of thy servant, and to the prayer of thy servants, who delight to fear thy name; and prosper, I pray thee, thy servant this day, and grant him mercy in the sight of [King Artaxerxes]. For I was the king's cupbearer. And it came to pass in the month Nisan, in the twentieth year of Artaxerxes, the king, that wine was before, hiet the king live forever. Why should not my countenance be sad, when the city, the place of my fathers' sepulchers, lieth waste, and its gates are consumed with fire? Then the king said unto me, For what dost thou make request? So I prayed to the God of heaven. And I said unto the king, If it please the king, and if thy servant hath found favor in thy sight, that thou wouldest send me unto Judah, unto the city of my fathers' sepulchers, that I may build it. And the king said unto me (the queen also sitting by him), For how long shall thy journey be? And when wilt thou return? So it pleased the king to send me, and I set him a time. Moreover, I said unto the king, If it please the king, let letters be given me to the governors beyond the river, that they may let me pass through till I come unto Judah; and a letter unto Asaph, the keeper of the king's forest, that he may give me timber to make beams for the gates of the palace which is near to the house, and for the wall of the city, and for the house that I shall enter into. And the king granted me, according to the good hand of my God upon me."

These passages document the prophecy and its fulfillment to the day over half a millennium, demonstrating the Spiritual capability of understanding time, including the future of the material world, more completely than in the material world, as well as influencing events in the material world.

Actually, the Bible is replete with such examples of Jesus and other inhabitants of the spiritual domain foretelling the future and exercising dominion over the material world, including Matthew 8:23-27, Matthew 17:24-27, Matthew 21:12 and 13, Matthew 22:29-32, Luke 1:26-38, Luke 24:1-32 and Luke 24:36-42. In 1 Corinthians 15:51-58 and elsewhere, Paul makes it plain that the spiritual domain is superior to and to be desired above the material world:

> "Behold, I show you a mystery: We shall not all sleep, but we shall all be changed, in a moment, in the twinkling of an eye, at the last trump; for the trumpet shall sound, and the dead shall be raised incorruptible, and we shall be changed. For this corruptible must put on incorruption, and this mortal must put on immortality. So, when this corruptible shall have put on incorruption, and this mortal shall have put on immortality, then shall be brought to pass the saying that is written, Death is swallowed up in victory. O death, where is thy sting? O grave, where is thy victory? The sting of death is sin; and the strength of sin is the law. But thanks be to God, who giveth us the victory through our Lord Jesus Christ. Therefore, my beloved brethren, be ye steadfast, unmovable, always abounding in the work of the Lord, forasmuch as ye know that your labor is not in vain in the Lord."

The bottom line in all of this is that the "material" domain which we now inhabit obviously is but a subset of the spiritual world. It's just a piece, and, from what Paul implies in his letters, it's a small one at that. Some theologians have gone so far as to declare that there seems to be some commonality between what we know about the spiritual domain and our observations at the atomic level regarding quantum physics, where interactions between objects can occur instantaneously, movement takes place in jumps, and observations impact what is being observed. What we know of the quantum world is so anti-intuitive that it seems utterly alien to our senses. In fact, outside of the nature of God there's nothing in our repertoire of knowledge about nature that comes close to what we observe in the domain of atoms and their components – except one genre of objects: UFOs, which opens the question as to whether they're related.

CHAPTER THREE

The Event

Returning to my own tale, the event itself occurred around ten o'clock one night in the fall of 1973 during a business trip from Bellevue, Washington to Eugene, Oregon. This time the travel was by car, the vehicle being my tired old Volkswagen Bug. I had been driving southward on I-5 toward Eugene with a companion, normally a draftsman, who would be occupied at our destination as an electrical technician. He'd be helping out with a problem we were experiencing with new equipment we had installed in Eugene. We saw a restaurant sign just off the freeway in Wilsonville, about ten miles south of Portland, and decided to stop there for a bite to eat. After we'd finished eating, we got into the car and headed back toward the freeway overpass to resume our southward journey.

We had just entered the overpass when my passenger thrust his arm across my face, pointing to the south. "Look!" he shouted in a rare display of emotion. As I turned my head toward his outstretched finger I caught a glimpse of an 18-wheeler in front, the truck skewed across the roadway ahead. The driver obviously was staring at the same sight. Turning my head southward, I saw what seemed to me to be an enormous disc-shaped object hovering near the next overpass about a mile south of ours. Being a certified flight instructor with enough hours of night flying to know what airplanes look like at night, both on the ground and in the air, I was startled at the size of this object. This craft was almost incomprehensibly huge, being very much larger than a Boeing 747. Returning my attention back to the roadway ahead, I threaded the car around the semi and hit the on-ramp with the gas pedal pressed to the floor. That didn't amount to much of a burst of speed, the car being what it was. I had timed its acceleration once – the 0-60 time neared 30 seconds. I imagine the occupants of the craft got a good laugh out of that. Nevertheless, the craft stayed motionless as we headed toward it, and I had another impression, one of three rectangular windows, the long sides vertical, and of being observed with an intensity of interest by someone – or thing – within.

As we got about halfway to the overpass near where it had remained in a stationary hover, the craft lifted, wobbled, and crossed over I-5 heading eastward very slowly, seeming to descend among the tall evergreen trees in the area. We exited the highway and headed eastbound after it, but by that time the craft was gone from our vision. We eventually gave up the chase and returned to the freeway toward our destination of Eugene, somewhat relieved to be getting back on track. We had been tired, having worked a full day back in the office before starting on the trip, and were looking forward to checking into a motel in Eugene and getting some sleep. Yet I remember having felt a sharp sense of loss as well, a keen disappointment over losing something that I had and was giving up.

Over time a vague uncertainty crept in as to whether that was the extent of the incident. We had checked the time when we broke off the chase. We apparently had been looking for the craft for about 45 minutes. At the time I thought nothing of it, but since then I've had a recurring thought that three quarters of an hour is a really long time to be looking for something, particularly when we were so close to our starting point near the freeway when we ended the chase. Nevertheless, I shoved that thought aside too, having more important things to think about.

We spent that weekend in Eugene on the job, and, returning Sunday, flipped a coin, the loser having to report the incident to the highway patrol. Having lost the toss, I made the call and was treated to the rudest response I have ever experienced this side of boot camp. I shrugged my shoulders and headed back northward, determined that I'd keep that kind of experience to myself, then and in the future.

CHAPTER FOUR

The Aftermath

The aftermath of my experience with the UFO sighting began about the same time I realized there was a connection with my understanding of the Bible. I had begun to pick up and read several popular Christian books, including Hal Lindsey's *Late, Great Planet Earth*. One book that captured my intense interest was *Nine O'Clock in the Morning*, written by Dennis Bennett of St. Luke's Episcopal Church in Ballard, Washington. In that book, Fr. Bennett wrote of the amazing inrush of the Holy Spirit upon Jesus' disciples at the first Pentecost following Jesus' crucifixion and resurrection. All Christians can have that same experience, Fr. Bennett claimed. All one had to do was ask and believe. As to the born-again experience, Scripture itself asserts in John 3 that the indwelling Holy Spirit is available to every Christian.

Nicodemus wasn't like most of the other Pharisees. He actually believed that Jesus was the Jews' expected Messiah. He had a question that was troubling him but, knowing the prevailing attitude among his peers, went to Jesus at night to avoid a confrontation with them. Jesus, knowing the question in Nicodemus' mind, answered him before he got the words out of his mouth. "You need to be born again in order to see the kingdom of God," he said to the man.

This answer only raised further issues with the confused man, who had insisted upon viewing the world through material rather than spiritual eyes. *How can a person possibly be born again?* He tried to picture the process. *Would he have to go back into his mother's womb? That doesn't make sense.*

Jesus replied with the assertion that the rebirth was spiritual rather than physical, and was accomplished by the Holy Spirit, who works as the

Father wills and can be seen primarily through the indwelling effect on persons.

The born-again experience has been well-known within the Christian community for a very long time, and now is largely taken for granted. Fr. Bennett, to his everlasting credit, reached beyond the low modern expectation of what that experience meant. He recalled the power that the indwelling Holy Spirit conferred upon the first Christians, asserting that this same power and the corresponding intimate love of God is still available to Christians at large. Scripture describes the overwhelming nature of this power in Acts Chapter 2, from which Bennett took the title of his book, *Nine O'Clock in the Morning.*

According to Moses in Leviticus 23, the Feast of Pentecost would take place fifty days after the waving of the sheaf offering representing the first fruits of the harvest. Jesus' resurrection represented the first fruit of God's harvest of souls. In line with that event, all of which was fulfilled in time according to the dates of the Mosaic feasts, the day of Pentecost following it occurred fifty days later. And it came in force like a mighty wind, indwelling the timid souls congregated in the upper room and endowing them with new and bold life. Some began to speak in tongues that were alien to them, but were readily understandable as their native languages to the diverse group of nearby devout foreigners.

There was such an uproar in all this that some people claimed that the disciples were drunk. Peter corrected the complainers, reminding them that it was only nine o'clock in the morning, much too early for them to be drinking. Instead, he told the crowd, the prophet Joel had foretold this very event in which God would pour out His Spirit upon them, causing sons and daughters to prophesy, young men to have visions, and old men to dream dreams. Furthermore, God would show signs in the heavens above, and whoever would call on the Lord would be saved.

The indwelling Holy Spirit transformed Peter from a willful, sometimes fearful person of the flesh into a giant man of God. He went on to do exploits, bringing the Word of salvation first to three thousand, then to five thousand, and after that to the entire Gentile world through Cornelius; calling upon the name of Jesus, he healed infirmities and restored the dead back to life. Two chapters of New Testament Scripture bear his name. Can this power of service to God actually be granted to us, two millennia later? Cessationists, drawing on one dubiously-interpreted passage in Scripture to excuse their own indifference and lack of faith, say no. To his great credit, Bennett said yes.

We did attend a Church that viewed the Holy Spirit in the same manner that Bennett did. It was of no small benefit to us that the Holy

Spirit did indeed choose to hit that Church with a very large dose of God's powerful, enabling presence. Our Church was overwhelmed with eager Christians, seeking and finding the Spirit of God. Soon, despite multiple services there was standing-room only within the Church, and the services had to be televised to the large crowd without. True miracles took place, and the power of God was revealed to the faithful in a way that had not been expected for centuries. The Church enjoyed a massive following for years thereafter.

Eventually, for reasons known only to God, the Holy Spirit chose to leave that Church in the manner of the wind spoken of by Jesus in John 3. That's when things turned sour there. The Church refused to accept the departure of the Holy Spirit, opting, as I suspect, to stretch the truth regarding the healings and empowerment of its member Christians. The desperate Church leaders begged the congregation to reclaim their spiritual heritage, insisting upon spiritual acquisition at the expense of Scripture itself. That's when I left.

Word got out of the miscreancy of this Church. Cessationists shouted "I told you so!" as if the visitation of the Holy Spirit had not happened at all. But it did. I was a witness and I saw that power, and I have experienced the aftermath of that as well.

CHAPTER FIVE

Further Experiences

Before leaving my charismatically-oriented Church, I had two follow-on experiences that will remain in my mind forever. Both of them had an enormous impact on my life.

A few months after starting to attend that Church I received a vision, perhaps the only one I'll ever have. It was an image of a very bleak, cold landscape, virtually empty of life. It wasn't just a cold area on earth; it was more like being surrounded with the implacable cold of interstellar space. Indeed, there was nothing there to support life, and it was far too frigid besides. Near the top of a cliff was a cave, and in that cave was a she-wolf in obvious distress, the cold harsh wind parting her fur in search of flesh to attack and freeze. Nevertheless, she remained completely still, as she was nursing a brood of cubs. The cubs themselves, nestling beneath her and being warmed and fed, were completely oblivious to their mother or the pain she was experiencing on their behalf. They fought each other for the best source of milk, suckling greedily.

The cubs, I was given to understand, were us. The she-wolf, I also was given to understand in that vision that was so emotionally real that it made me weep, represented the Holy Spirit.

Not long after that first experience associated with the Church, the pastoral staff held a special baptismal service to which my wife at the time, our two daughters, and I came to attend. It was a typical Seattle day, cloudy with sun breaks.

As we waited in our pew for our turn to be baptized, I looked up at the altar. Behind the altar was a very large window of colored glass. The colors were arranged to depict Jesus. I marveled at the glow on Jesus' face as the sun shone on that window. As we were next in line, my attention turned to the baptism proceedings. As my family was being baptized, I happened to look up again toward the altar. This time a cloud had covered the sun. Jesus' face was dark. That may have been a coincidence, but the association gave me a deep sorrow. Later I would have cause to revisit that foreboding in my mind.

PART TWO

A CALL TO ACTION

CHAPTER SIX

Being Led by God

Although I didn't recognize it at the time, while we were attending the Church that was so devoted to the Holy Spirit, the aftermath of the life-changing Christian conversion began to impact our lives in radical new ways.

Having been urged by God, who also supplied the much-needed courage and compassion to follow through with the gentle command, my wife and I found ourselves in the parking lot of a nursing home that was located near where we lived. The facility was devoted to the care of handicapped persons, most of whom were children whose daily needs exceeded the capacity of their parents to provide for them.

We stayed in the car for several minutes, stalling off the frightening prospect our next move would fulfill. We had been brought up with thoroughly secular values. But here we neophytes in the faith were being asked by God to impart to others less fortunate than ourselves the knowledge of Scripture that had been given me at the time of the event of which I write. Attending to the Christian instruction of handicapped inmates was so far off our normal routine that we couldn't imagine doing it of our own volition.

Eventually we ran out of excuses to stay in the car. Gritting our teeth, we traversed the asphalt parking lot and entered the building, where we were instantly assaulted by the smell of urine. A worker was in the process of mopping up a puddle, but the odor was more pervasive than that wet spot possibly could generate. As we walked across the cheap linoleum floor to a reception area the noise began to intrude upon the signals from our noses, which were beginning to accommodate to the new environment. There was an indistinct background hum generated by a multitude of inmates, some of the closer who emitted groans and wails. The noise was soon overwhelmed by the visual impact of wheelchair-bound bodies whose limbs assumed grotesque angles, signaling the nature of the prevailing affliction, which was cerebral palsy.

We were greeted with indifference by the receptionist. "What do you want?" she asked. Stumbling for words, I finally told her that we were here to volunteer with a Bible study. She looked us over with a bold, accusing stare and finally broke eye contact. "Wait one," she said, and turned to her phone. She ignored us after that, but we had heard from her end of the conversation that she had asked the Activities Director to come to the front desk. My wife looked at me and slowly shook her head. We almost left at that point, but before we took action Mary was in front of us. Having been charmed by her warm, understanding smile, we opened up to her, explaining what we had intended to do. She accepted our intentions as honorable, but explained that the first step was a necessary background check. We gave her the information she asked for, after which she told us that we'd hear from her within the week. As we exited the building, we drew breaths of fresh air with great relief.

Throughout the next week we were plagued with conflict. One moment we'd be ready to cancel out on the commitment and the next we'd be looking forward to Mary's answer, for which we'd have to wait until the end of the week. The answer came in the form of a question. Asking if we could provide a Bible study on Sunday evening, she told us that we'd be filling a vacancy in that area that had persisted for far too long. Given her positive, friendly call, our enthusiasm picked up. We agreed whole-heartedly to a Bible study.

That Sunday evening we began a weekly Bible study that continued for four years. With my wife joining in with the piano, we would spend the evening singing hymns and reading from the Bible. Eventually I learned to look past the disabilities to the persons inside, and began to bond with a young fellow named Danny. Danny was so severely afflicted with cerebral palsy that he couldn't speak intelligently or move his arms or legs in any semblance of order or purpose. But he had a sunny disposition and a sense of adventure that the Holy Spirit made sure that I would become aware of. I vividly remember the Sunday afternoon that I came early to spend some time with him on a stroll through the grounds of a nearby park. As I pushed his wheelchair along the walkway we came upon a dip in the path. At that point I let go and told Danny to "go for it". I'll always remember his happy face as he struggled to pump his fist in affirmation. I had no idea at the time that this tiny incident would lead to such an amazing adventure. But God certainly knew: this was just one little episode in a much larger event that God was carefully orchestrating.

CHAPTER SEVEN

Following God into Adventure

I always have loved adventure, and I loved to fly. Though my career was in electrical engineering, I had dreams of some day becoming an airline pilot, and worked to fulfill that dream by acquiring ratings through the G. I. Bill. It was not to be. Not very long after obtaining what were the necessary prerequisite instructor, commercial, instrument and multi-engine ratings, I was denied through a hearing issue a medical certificate appropriate for commercial operations. Moreover, I was prevented from benefiting financially from my commercial and instructor ratings. Faced with the steeply-rising cost of aircraft rentals, I gave up flying in favor of less expensive pursuits.

At the time of our nursing home Bible study it had been years since I had flown an airplane. Those long years later my dear brother Jon resurrected the flying activity at a more basic level by gifting me with lessons in hang gliding. As he told me then, he had seen training activity near where he lived, and the thought of me stumbling and raising dust in imperfect landings appealed to his sense of humor. I knew that he was simply covering up for an act of compassion toward his brother. But the stumbling part was very real, at least for me, and it appealed as well to my own sense of humor. The beginning student is either subjected or treated, depending on how he looks at it, to a relentless series of dustups, crashes, and general disasters before he acquires the hang of hang flight. If one sees the humor in the experience, as I did even though I was forty one years old and starting to feel the pain of falling, the hilarity is cosmic. Later, as I gained experience in and had tamped down my early fear of stepping off cliffs, I became even more enamored with it: scenes of exquisite oneness with my Dacron wings above pristine wilderness are indelibly embedded in my psyche. The accidents and near-accidents also reside in my brain, but I view them with good humor as well.

What I didn't understand at the time was that my hang gliding activity would intersect with our nursing home activity and particularly with Danny in the most unexpected and amazing way. One day, as I was flying, I suddenly recalled Danny's look of excitement when I had let go of his wheelchair at the dip in the path. *Wouldn't it be great,* I thought, *if Danny could join me in flight.* My first thought after that was *Well, maybe not me, but somebody younger and with more experience.*

It was especially difficult at first to picture why God would get involved in such a trivial objective. The idea of God even being interested in hang gliding was beyond the scope of my understanding. What I had failed to grasp was God's infinite compassion toward a young man whose body prevented him from pursuing the smallest dream so common to normal youth. Danny had a fully-functional brain. He was probably smarter than me. His physical handicap only emphasized the denial to him of the joy of normal living.

I know that at times Christians are asked to suffer in some manner, either physically or emotionally or both. In that context, Philippians 1:29 sticks in my mind. In that passage Paul claims that it is given to Christians not only to believe on Him, but also to suffer for his sake. If one attempts to attach a different meaning to that very straightforward message, there are other passages, such as in Hebrews 11 and 12 and 1 Peter, that say essentially the same thing, and would have to be dealt with as well.

Not all Christians, as I see it, are called to suffer in the same manner or to the same extent. Only God knows why that is, but I do know that we are not called to suffer out of God's anger or hatred, but of love. God said as much in Hebrews 12:5-11, where is speaks of a person who does not undergo chastisement as a bastard rather than a legitimate kin. I think that a big reason for this is that God wishes to prepare our characters to fully appreciate and enjoy the love that will be bestowed upon us in our marriage to Jesus in the spiritual realm. In my mind, God wishes to impart to us a nobility fitting for that relationship, whether we like it or not.

In those difficult passages that speak of chastisement we may get a glimpse of the beauty of our maternal Holy Spirit as She indwells us to comfort us as would a mother to reconcile the loving nature of God with the suffering that the believer must face to strip him of his selfishness and thus render him capable of the love necessary for him to enjoy full communication and companionship with God.

I fervently hope that our beloved Holy Spirit had indwelt Danny in that manner. I have reason to believe, from the following account, that the Holy Spirit did just that and more with Danny, using him as well in a mighty way to display the compassion of God to the hang gliding community and its attendant community of onlookers.

As for the God's interaction with me, I can claim with the authority of personal experience the comfort offered by the Holy Spirit in the face of discomfort from outside. In the example I give below, the main discomfort was the overcoming of fear. The unease was so strong that I can't conceive of myself doing on my own what God had me do for the sake of another individual.

Here I'll boast on the Lord and do so happily. If He has used me, it gladdens me that He saw fit to do so, for the chance to participate in God's work is infinitely better than personal accomplishment. Were it not for Paul's statement in 1 Corinthians 1:26-31, I'd be tempted to brag a bit about some of my experiences, but this particular passage goes a long way toward putting me in my place. Paul's words are far more eloquent than any that I could come up with myself:

> "For ye see your calling, brethren, how that not many wise men after the flesh, not many mighty, not many noble, are called; but God hath chosen the foolish things of the world to confound the wise; and God hath chosen the weak things of the world to confound the things which are mighty; and base things of the world, and things which are despised, hath God chosen, yea, and things which are not, to bring to nought things that are, that no flesh should glory in his presence. But of him are ye in Christ Jesus, who of God is made unto us wisdom, and righteousness, and sanctification, and redemption; that, according as it is written, He that glorieth, let him glory in the Lord."

That passage simply reinforces what I already know about myself. I have always been aware of my own intellectual disability: I'm a slow learner. My slowness, unfortunately, extends to my body as well. I was never cut out to be a star athlete or a star anything that requires a quick eye and speed of response. The hearing issue that prevented me from remaining a commercial pilot has been a blessing to all the lives that I'd have endangered in the process of taking to the sky with them as paying passengers. However, as I was soon to find out, with God all things are possible.

CHAPTER EIGHT

Journeys into the Unknown

Regarding the involvement of God in our nursing home activity, my young friend Harold helped me accomplish a task of such personal importance that I won't forget it as long as I live. But now I fully appreciate that it was the loving Holy Spirit who had guided us both.

Faced with a knowledge of my own limitations along with a persistent urge to include Danny in the joy of flight, I approached several pilots who were far younger and had more air time than I did. But I was turned down flat. The manner in which they responded hinted that the idea was an affront: they couldn't comprehend why a severely handicapped person should be on the big hill. Realizing that if anyone was going to do the job it would have to be me, for the next several months I worked hard on the big training hill at acquiring the necessary experience. At an elevation of a thousand feet above the farmland terrain below it and a steepness of slope that approached the nature of a true cliff, the big hill would have been considered by many to be an ideal site not only for beginners but for all levels of experience. Indeed, it was used by many competent local pilots for recreation as much as for gaining experience. Its ideal situation for training and its drawback for general recreation was its orientation and the weather patterns of Western Washington State that precluded updrafts of either ridge-lift or thermal origin. I once managed to rise above launch there on a rare thermal, but the altitude gain was paltry and short-lived.

Toward the end of that time of training, I had Danny weighed at 94 pounds and took to the big hill wearing a backpack into which I inserted a progressively increasing number of lead SCUBA weights. I had gotten up to about 60 pounds when I really began to worry about overstressing my glider. About that time also my flying friends, including Harold, were venturing farther afield with their gliders in search of better lift conditions. Not willing to be left behind on the big hill, I went along with them, essentially putting the project with Danny on hold.

I had nothing to do with what happened next. It just came about without one speck of input from me. One morning a few months after putting the idea of Danny flying on hold something happened right out of the blue that changed my life the instant that I woke up. When I did awake it was to a strange peace and the certain knowledge – it wasn't just a feeling, but a deeply rooted understanding - that on that day I would take Danny up to the big hill and we would jump off together. I had no idea how that might be done, but I was sure that it would, despite the fact that I had never flown in a glider with another person, even as a passenger, and had no idea what to expect. I now cherish this knowledge and especially the peace regarding it as a gift from the Holy Spirit. Every year that passes I am more certain of this fact. And I'm very grateful about it.

The first thing I did after getting dressed was to call Harold, asking him to come with me and help to figure out how we were going to get Danny into the air. Then I went to the nursing home, told the staff what I intended to do, and picked up Danny. I doubt if I'd get away with that now, but things were looser back then. Maybe the Holy Spirit had something to do with their attitude as well. We met up with Harold on the big hill, where he was already trying to figure out how the launch was going to take place. He had a rope slung over his shoulder when Danny and I arrived and was eyeing a big stump. He wrapped the end of the rope around the stump as I came up to him, and walked over to the edge. "I think this is gonna work," he said as he wrapped the other end around his waist, cinching it tightly. "Go ahead and set up," he continued as he tested it. He had just enough slack to get him over the edge at a 45 degree angle.

Harold had the compassion and strength and most of all the courage to be an ideal companion for this project. As I walked the glider to where I'd run off the edge, Harold cradled Danny in his harness. We hooked him into the keel, along with me, while he continued to hold Danny in his arms. When I signaled my intent to go, he ran with me to the edge and, just as he felt the tug of the rope around his waist, flung him away as the glider left the ground.

I felt a twist of Danny's harness on the keel and, having not quite achieved flying speed, we momentarily dove in dubious control. But we had a thousand feet to sort things out, and eventually gained a semblance of normal flight. By this time I was able to read Danny's expressions. As we floated above the farmland below he looked around to the ground beneath us, to the horizon to the front and to his hands on the basetube as if to capture every aspect of this experience in his memory. His excitement was extreme, his jaw dropping as he attempted to grin, and it gave me a wonderful feeling that this strange thing we were doing was being smiled upon by God. This feeling of euphoria continued after we landed, when Danny gave me a look of pure joy.

After our first landing Danny was totally pumped. He flung his arms akimbo and strained to speak. I understood him as clearly as if his speech was perfect. Harold and I were both pumped too. It probably was the most significant moment of my life. No bones were broken, Danny and I were alive, Harold hadn't fallen off the cliff and we had acquired the experience of a successful venture. We could, in fact, do it again, and now without the fear of the unknown.

Harold and I were so excited about the successful flight that we decided to play this adventure out some more. Grinning stupidly, we said to each other "Let's do it again!"

We returned to the top of the big hill and set up the glider once more. Harold wrapped the rope around his waist, tugged on it, and took Danny and his harness in his arms. I signaled and began to run, and Harold followed and flung Danny off.

Unfortunately, it being later in the day, the wind had changed from the usual weak updraft to a firmer downdraft. That situation is about the first thing that hang gliding instructors warn their students about, usually expressing the importance of it by shouting: "Don't launch downwind! It won't work!" I had checked it before launching, and knew about it but the success of the earlier flight crowded out rational thought. As I was soon reminded, human power is notoriously weak. The hang glider pilot needs all the help he can get to attain flying speed. Anything less results in a stall, which means that gravity rules over everything else.

True to form, there we were, heading downward in a stall. Theoretically, we had a thousand feet to sort things out and recover. The cliff, however, had a prominent ledge a couple of hundred feet down. Trees resided on the ledge. Big trees, over a hundred feet tall. By the time Danny and I had attained flying speed, we found ourselves below the treetops and heading rapidly toward them. Most fortunately, the wing itself remained above the tops and our combined mass was sufficient to plow through them. We were through the gauntlet, and after that the flight was uneventful. But we didn't fly any more that day.

The next flight didn't work out too well either. The flight itself was fine, but my landing lacked perfection. I was too low in the flare-out, just about kissing the grass. Danny's chin was lower yet. When he gets excited he drops his jaw. When we land he remains prone, thus making his jaw the lowest part of his body and, in actuality, the entire hang glider system. This would have been acceptable if the field contained nothing but grass. But it didn't. Cows grazed there. They ate the grass. They did other things on it, too, so it was inevitable that Danny's jaw would scoop up a cow pie.

It wasn't as funny as it sounds. He was choking and I was terrified that he wouldn't be able to breathe. As soon as I could I scrambled to clear his airway by poking my finger into his throat and pulling out the poop. His gasps reassured me that he was able to breathe, and I continued to kneel there, thanking God for His mercy in the face of my stupidity.

When we returned to the nursing home I felt compelled to tell the nurses about what had happened, because I wasn't sure that he wouldn't need a shot of something to immunize him against infection. The fact that Danny was there and he was alive and apparently in good spirits lightened up the situation considerably. They asked if there were flies on the poop. When I replied in the negative, they said that there was no real problem. Then they began to laugh. They were still laughing as I left the building.

We had four more flights together after that, three of which were made without untoward incidents. But I still shudder with the creeps when I remember the next flight.

To this point we had one very successful flight together, followed by two more somewhat marginal ones. The next flight was marginal too. In fact, it was the scariest of the lot. As before, Harold ran next to me with Danny, flinging him into the air as I reached the edge of the big hill. This time there was an added spin to the thrust, causing Danny's right arm to loop around the left flying wire that ran between the left tip of my crosstube and the left tip of my basetube.

If Danny's arm had been capable of flexing at the elbow, this wouldn't have mattered. The arm simply would have slipped back down, allowing Danny's harness to come back alongside mine when I went prone and put my hands on the basetube for control.

But Danny's arm was rigid at both elbow and shoulder, causing him to remain where he was, on the left side of the glider rather far away from the basetube.

If hang gliders had control surfaces common to airplanes like rudders and ailerons, that might not have been so terribly important. But hang gliders are controlled in flight by weight-shift, making control surfaces unnecessary under most conditions. Therefore, most hang gliders don't have control surfaces.

As didn't we. There we were then, flying marginally above stall speed with the glider sensing Danny's position as a rather stern command for a sharp left turn. A sharp left turn at that point would have brought us back toward our launch point. The problem with that, of course, is that now we were well below the launch point. As we began to turn, the cliff face came back into sight. It wasn't a pretty picture. Although he was fully aware of the situation, Danny's handicap prevented him from moving his arm. His frustration was extreme, matching the intensity of my own terror.

I had no choice. Tugging on the right flying wire, I pulled myself (scrabbled would be more accurate) out to the right to compensate for Danny's position. We straightened out and I was then able to turn us away from the cliff and back into unobstructed airspace. But in that position my control was marginal, especially with respect to pitch. We were flying, but barely. Setting up for a landing and then executing it without compromising our health would be extremely difficult under those conditions.

When we had enough room to recover from a complete loss of control, I took a few deep breaths to calm myself and let go from my precarious but relatively stable perch, swinging over toward Danny. As the glider, under our combined weight on the left side, began a turn again to the left, this time more abruptly than the last, I reached out and attempted to unhook the arm. Failing to do it, I scrambled back to the right just as the glider began its entry into what may well have been a terminal spiral.

Noting with dismay that we were closer to the ground and were approaching the point where we'd have insufficient altitude to recover from that kind of attitude, I took a few more deep breaths, prayed for God's help and repeated the maneuver. Spurred on by desperation, I did so more boldly than during my previous attempt. This time we were successful. We returned to stable flight greatly relieved and breathing heartfelt thanks to God for getting us out of that situation. The landing turned out to be good. It was the prayer that did it.

Danny and I, with Harold's continued help, had three more flights after that. They all were relatively uneventful. Then a number of significant events occurred in my life, all of which were unrelated to Danny, but which conspired against any further launches with him.

It was an experience that I'll never forget, not for the scares, but for the joy of the doing. I don't think Danny will, either. I suppose that I could feel guilty about having exposed Danny to such danger. But, given that he survived intact, his life ended up being far more meaningful than it otherwise would have been. I'm sure that Danny would agree to that also. Besides, God was in charge all the time.

Focused as we were on the task at hand, neither Harold nor I had noticed the number of onlookers to that first launch with Danny. One lady with a camera was standing on the edge of the cliff below Harold and snapped a picture just as we launched off. She was kind enough later to give me a copy, which I have very much appreciated. Over the years those events have taken over a surreal quality. Sometimes I look at that picture to confirm that it really happened as my memory struggles to recall. It's also on the front cover of my novel *Buddy*, which integrates that adventure, in fictional form, into a tale of God's compassionate healing of situations and people who appear to be beyond help.

The initial motivation for the novel *Buddy* and its sequels *Cathy, Jacob* and *Home, Sweet Heaven* arose from my first-hand witness of that loving compassion. I was influenced as well by its prime source, the feminine image of the Holy Spirit of which I spoke earlier. But first I had to go through a deep, heart-wrenching darkness of soul.

PART THREE

A TIME OF DARKNESS

Chapter Nine

Sorrow at Home

At the time that Harold and I were showing the sky to Danny, my joy was tempered with a situation that I was consciously trying very hard to deny. Yet it was intruding into my subconscious mind and bringing to the surface the foreboding that I had felt sometimes in my glimpses of the conversation I had had during the event with the UFO, and more overtly in flashbacks to the darkened face of Jesus during the baptism of my family.

I had met my wife in high school, and had kept a running communication by letter with her during my enlistment in the Marine Corps. A year after my enlistment ended and while I was in college we married. She was 18 and I was 19. Neither of us had any idea what marriage really involved, particularly the sacrifices from both partners that the union required. Nevertheless, we remained married through the ups and downs of my engineering career and the birth of our two lovely daughters.

As we embarked on our new Church-oriented lives I saw but refused to see a growing discontent on her part. It eventually flared up and failed to return to some semblance of normalcy. After nearly twenty-four years of marriage our marriage came to an end, and we parted ways.

There is a beautiful passage in Genesis, repeated by Jesus in Matthew 19 and by Paul in Ephesians 5, that describes a marriage in terms of union:

"Therefore shall a man leave his father and his mother, and shall cleave unto his wife; and they shall be one flesh."

This union includes the obvious sexual pairing, but represents far more than that. As the normal marriage matures in love, neurons and synapses form in the brain that imprint each partner into the other, forming in them a truly inseparable and complementary union.

As my wife and I parted company, all those neurons acquired over twenty-three years of marriage remained connected, but were denied the reinforcing physical presence of my former partner. Their disconnection was a slow and excruciating process that took years to accomplish. The rejection made it worse.

During the first few months after our breakup I was a basket case. I was barely able to accomplish the work required of my engineering position, and would return to my bleak little apartment to spend most of my evening weeping. One endless, agonizing day followed another in miserable, hopeless and lonely sequence. I begged God to somehow put me three years into the future, assuming that by then at least some of my sorrow would have been healed by the passage of time.

CHAPTER TEN

God Provides a Partner

God didn't do that. He did something far better. Through someone else's pain of a similar nature, He fashioned a new partner for me.

At the same time as I was experiencing the loss of my former wife, Carolyn was undergoing a parallel experience with her husband. They had been married for eighteen years and shared two lovely daughters of their own. Carolyn had been brought up in a rural town that held to traditional values that she had accepted as her own. Their final breakup occurred before our own, but not by very much.

Desperate for some company after a few weeks of misery, I started going to a nearby Church. Amazingly, it was one of those rare ones that had an active singles group. Soon I was taking part in the Bible-oriented Wednesday evening meetings, and found some very warm and welcoming people, all of whom had endured experiences like mine. The Bible study wasn't trivial; my new friends went deeply into Scripture, and my communion with God, which had suffered in the immediate aftermath of our breakup, was restored.

Several weeks later one of the men I'd befriended at the singles group called after work, demanding rather urgently that I come to the group's volleyball game that same evening. I had had a full day at work and was tired. The last thing I wanted to do was go to a sporting event in which my slow and awkward body probably would disgrace me among people I had just met. I started to decline but he insisted, saying that there weren't enough people without me to make up a decent game. I acquiesced very reluctantly. After a simple meal, I put on some shorts, a T-shirt and tennis shoes, and plodded off to the game.

I was a little late. The fellow who had called me came in later. He brought with him a cheerful lady, a person whom I thought might be his love interest. We played on opposite sides, where I was captivated by her lovely smile. *He's a lucky guy,* I thought to myself. I was distracted by the fact that she seemed to be focused on me rather than the fellow she'd come in with.

After the game was over we all piled onto the Church bus and headed to a nearby eatery. During the ride my confusion increased, as her partner for the evening wasn't exactly her partner. He had his arms around the shoulders of another lady. It finally dawned on me, as I overheard another nearby conversation, that this lady who had been smiling at me during the game was his sister! Armed with that revelation, I became more aggressive, making sure that I was seated next to her at the table where we ordered snacks and appetizers. We had a delightful conversation.

I learned later from her brother that he'd been eying me for a couple of weeks as a possible candidate for his sister's affections. He said that God had kind of rushed it, moving him to invite his sister to the volleyball game. She didn't share his plans. She lived some distance from that place, had to work early the next morning, and just wasn't up to meeting someone new. She'd had it with men since her breakup with her husband; they all seemed to want only a casual relationship. Thanks, but no thanks, she told her brother. I don't know the details of their follow-on conversation, but evidently he was very insistent. She reluctantly agreed to go to the game, but only if he picked her up and returned her home in time for a decent night's sleep.

Two weeks after the game, with prayer to God I screwed up my courage and asked her out on a date, which happened to be a trip to the top of Snoqualmie Pass to ski. Our time together in the lodge after the skiing was so good that we both became interested in pursuing the relationship.

My breakup with my former wife had taken so much wind out of my sails that it effectively ended my adventures with Danny, and the Bible study as well. But a new adventure came in its place: on our second date a couple of weeks after the first, I took Carolyn up to the big hill and we took off together on the hang glider. After our sixth such flight she looked up to me after we landed and said "When are we going to get some real air time?" I later learned that she was speaking from a good dose of pure bravado, but I was impressed at the time. I took her up on that soon after that, taking her up to Dog Mountain near the towns of Morton and Glenoma. Dog Mountain is another popular hang gliding site that also enjoys a large number of days where the wind endows it with ridge lift. Ridge lift lets the pilot remain aloft for substantial amounts of time.

Carolyn had asked for it, and now she got it. We launched off together in the morning and tooled around above the mountain for almost an hour, during which Carolyn truly enjoyed the experience. Eventually the turbulence gave her a bout of airsickness. Reluctantly, we came down to a landing. When she recovered we enjoyed a nice chicken dinner at the home of an onlooker who lived nearby.

Our relationship was progressing faster than either of us wanted, particularly with children in the mix. Both of us were still grieving from the abrupt end of our former marriages, and our recovery from that loss would still take time. I decided to move down to California and take a job with a friend.

We were separated physically for almost a year, but had continued to communicate by letter and telephone. That was long enough. We married the next year, beginning a union that has been blessed far beyond our expectations. In our 34 years of marriage since then, we've had adventures and made memories that we would only have dreamed about in our former marriages, and have developed into a union that is quite extraordinarily close and loving.

By the time we returned from California to Washington, our marriage and our children had demanded more of our time – much more. Something had to give, and it was the hang glider. I was working two jobs as well, trying to meet the additional burden of child support and mortgage payments on my former house. For a year or two, we remained tied somewhat tightly to our home, a beautiful house owned by Carolyn that I had known nothing about until we were well along in our relationship. We had tried to sell the home while we were in California, intending to stay in that state. Nothing seemed to work in that direction, and when we returned to Washington, we were very appreciative of God for nixing that plan.

After her breakup with her former husband, Carolyn had rented the house out and moved into an apartment into Tacoma. That was the context in which our relationship grew. When we moved into the house after returning from California, we found quite soon that the renters had done an abominable job of maintaining it and the yard. All our efforts in our free time were devoted to restoring her home to some semblance of its former glory.

Chapter Eleven

A New Adventure

One such time of heavy yard work turned out to be a nudge into another adventure. It was an unusually hot day for the Northwest, and I was laboring in the yard, pick in hand with a bare chest covered in sweat. Along came one of our daughters' boyfriends on his shiny new motorcycle, a 750 cc Yamaha Maxim. I looked at it longingly. The last time I had ridden a motorcycle was in college, to where I had commuted in my Triumph 650. The boyfriend was insufferably cocky and he had no idea that the grey-haired man looking over his bike had any experience on one. I finally asked him, "Would you mind it I drove it for a very short time to cool off?"

His response was a grinning "Go for it, pops." I think he was waiting for me to crash and burn, giving him the opportunity to collect on the damage for repairs to a bike he couldn't afford in the first place.

As soon as I got on I didn't want to get off. When I returned, the owner's face showed disappointment in the intact bike, but brightened again when I asked if I could buy it. After hearing the price he wanted, I talked it over with Carolyn. I thought she'd say no, but surprisingly she asked to have a ride first to see what she thought of being a passenger. I put on a shirt and we took off together on the bike to a distant restaurant, our daughter and her boyfriend following in her car. By the time we got to the restaurant Carolyn was hooked as well. We bought Ol' Betsy for far too much, which made the boyfriend think he'd just found the Mother Lode, and since that time made some epic trips on her. Our first trip was an ambitious one that took us from Washington to New Mexico by way of Idaho, Montana and Colorado.

The ride to New Mexico was romantic as well as ambitious. And it came with a fair share of negatives, which for the most part simply added color. However, I should color one incident a dark grey, perhaps almost black. It was all my fault. The Yamaha was so-so on the passenger's comfort, particularly the seat. Soon after riding with me Carolyn had established one iron-clad rule: stop the bike at least every two hours to give her rear end a rest. Once on the trip I forgot to do that, an oversight of which Carolyn reminded me with her fists in my kidneys. As soon as I had stopped she jumped off, flung her helmet off into the field next to the highway and started walking. After retrieving the helmet, I putt-putted the bike on the shoulder next to her, begging her to forgive me and get back on. By that time she was crying, big crocodile tears out of her red eyes. The sight of my pleading face near her weeping one attracted the attention of all the vehicles coming toward us. Some honked; others openly laughed, and all were grinning one way or another. Eventually she decided that my humiliation was complete enough that she relented and got back on. "Never, NEVER do that again," she shouted in my ear. I didn't – until the next time it happened, which is a different story. That night I stopped at an upscale motel in Pocatello and treated her to a lavish dinner and movie. The next day Carolyn's anger regarding my ill-mannered behavior in not giving her the rest she needed was replaced by some unexpected cowboy excitement when we found ourselves in the middle of a cattle drive. We felt like we were part of the team doing the herding.

That day we continued on into Colorado, where we stopped for the night at Glenwood Springs, which has become one of our favorite stopover places. We stayed at the Hotel Colorado, an old but very charming hotel that President Theodore Roosevelt frequented and which was temporarily used as a recovery center for wounded soldiers in World War II. The grounds were beautiful, and adjoined an immense pool fed by a natural hot spring. Surrounding the pool was a lovely expanse of grass where we enjoyed reading in between dips. We had known that we shared a passion for reading, but on that trip we discovered that our books were all the entertainment we needed during our leisure time – it was sufficient for us to just be next to each other while we enjoyed our novels.

We were simply unable to leave the next morning. Had we been less ambitious, we would have stayed right there until it was time to return home. Indeed, Glenwood Springs became our destination for two other trips. As it was, we stayed on for another day, and then continued our southward journey, reaching the top of Independence Pass some time around noon. We took a southeastward tack from there running into hail that obscured the Sangre de Cristo mountains to the east. That night we stayed at Alamosa near the Rio Grande River, where it was raining heavily. We turned in to a campground that belonged to a well-known chain and set up our tent at the assigned spot. Not much later that night, we awoke to two inches of water inside our tent. Our assigned spot turned out to be a swamp. Unable to sleep any more, we gathered up our dripping paraphernalia and left the campground, which we were happy to see in our sideview mirrors. It definitely was not a destination resort, but we had been so charmed by the new sights and our first bike trip that we simply considered it to be another adventure. Fortunately the rain had stopped, so we didn't get any wetter than we were. We crossed the Rio Grande in the dark and entered New Mexico. That morning we checked in to a motel in a little town called Espanola, draped our still-wet sleeping bag and tent over the shower and turned up the heat. We didn't need a room number. All we had to do was look up from the parking lot and see the room with the fogged windows. We stayed until our gear dried out, but were happy to do so, as we took our meals in one of the best Mexican restaurants we'd ever come across.

We continued southward as far as Santa Fe, and then headed upward into the mountains. At the famous little town of Taos we stopped briefly to admire the beautiful paintings of some of the very talented local artists. Continuing on up the mountain, we found ourselves at the ten thousand-foot level in the midst of a beautiful ski area. Pitching our tent in a campground nearby, we had a memorable dinner at Texas Red's, where we made a rather large contribution to the peanut shells on the floor.

I'll wind up here on the description of our travels, lest this book should turn into a travelogue. It would be sufficient to say that this trip was just one of a great many wonderful adventures that Carolyn and I shared together. In fact, our marriage itself has been a grand adventure that included many bike trips, two of which were cross-country. There were a number of boats involved as well, one of which was a beautiful sailboat that offered us such a richness of memories that we gladly put up for a time with the financial disaster that it represented.

True to the warning I had been given during the event that changed my life, I did indeed suffer a period of darkness. Carolyn did as well. For both of us, it was a heartbreaking experience. At the time it seemed as if our lives were over, that what remained of them would be a continuum of bleak and empty days and nights.

Now, as I look back on the thirty four years to date of my marriage to Carolyn and the romance that it has entailed, I can truly say that when our troubles came, our lives were just beginning. Compared with the wonder of our shared lives, the period of darkness was so slight as to be insignificant. Both of us can truly agree with Paul in Romans 8:28:

> *"And we know that all things work together for good to them that love God, to them who are the called according to his purpose."*

Having had a taste of the benevolence of our God, we look forward to an earlier passage in Romans 8, verse 18:

> *"For I reckon that the sufferings of this present time are not worthy to be compared with the glory which shall be revealed in us."*

I have no idea whether the darkness we have already experienced will be the last for us. Regardless, the light of Jesus Christ has shone brightly in our lives to date, and we eagerly await the time that we shall see our Lord face-to-face.

Our adventures in the Word of God have extended far beyond the experiences noted above. The thrill of discovering the nature of God that included a happy struggle to comprehend Jesus' feeding events has led to an unexpected career of writing about Him. To date, this occupation has resulted in two Christian nonfiction books, *Family of God* and *Marching to a Worthy Drummer*, as well as the *Buddy* series of four novels, *Buddy, Cathy, Jacob,* and *Home, Sweet Heaven.*

CHAPTER TWELVE

God's Nobility

I am convinced that there are two basic reasons why some individuals view Jesus as less than God or irrelevant to our modern world. The reasons are related. The first reason I would offer is simple ignorance of Scripture, at least in the depth in which it was intended to be digested. Primarily, however, ignorance of Scripture usually comes from an indifference toward it. That relates to the second reason for perceiving a human Jesus: some people simply don't want to see God. If people with this attitude read Scripture at all, they are motivated by a desire to support their *a priori* conviction that it is not inspired by God.

But why would someone not want to see God? Having been on both sides of that particular fence, my personal understanding is that God gets in the way of self. Self and ego demand independence from the control of God. It is far more comfortable to the selfish narcissist to believe that nothing but goodness and pleasure can be extracted from this world if one plays his cards right.

Rejection is an evil thing, but it does have its uses. Even during the worst of it, my time of darkness wasn't all negative. It was, in fact, a necessary element of my growth as a Christian. Through it I acquired some much-needed humility. The stark fact of rejection allowed for no rationalization. It stood there unmoving, staring me in the face, and it humbled me. But through that process of reduction I learned to get over myself, which permitted me to place my ego at the feet of Jesus.

In *Marching to a Worthy Drummer* I expanded on my discussion in *Family of God* of this enormously important issue of evil in the face of God's goodness. In that book I identified the ultimate ride as not a ride but rather the lifestyle of the fully-committed Christian. Being an outsider to Christianity for half of my life and knowing full well how the outsider views the Christian lifestyle, I noted that while to the outsider the Christian life looks impossibly bleak it really is anything but that to the earnest Christian. Having been challenged by more than one relative to answer why, if our God is so good, bad things happen to "good" people, I responded that the question was intended to demonstrate that the disconnect between God and harshness that some people experience in life represents a paradox that suggests that God doesn't really exist. I went on to point to the amazing supernatural track record of Scriptural prophecy's historical fulfillment, and then turned to the behavioral nature of the argument that God didn't exist, pointing to the declaration in 1 John 4:7-10 that God represents the essence of love, reminding my relative that God loved us with such passion that He sent His beloved Son to die in our place for the sins that we have committed, and that He did so before we loved Him. I linked that attribute with the noble, selfless nature of the Holy Spirit.

I told my relative to read what I had written about love in the presence of evil in the chapter entitled "The Utility of Evil" in my book *Family of God*. When I eventually heard back from him, I was surprised by his subdued attitude. He acknowledged that it made sense that a person has to experience the effect of evil to appreciate the goodness of God, to which I replied in the affirmative with the caution that this notion was only a small part of the answer. I told him that an important part of the picture is that we don't live for ourselves. Having been created by God, we do indeed live for Him, but that this connection is love-centered in which God wishes to have a loving relationship with us. Eventually, according to Ephesians 5:31 and 32, we as the composite Church will be the bride of Jesus, a relationship that calls for our development from our basically self-centered natures into a selfless nobility fitting for that future relationship. Those who are mentally and emotionally bogged down in our limited physical universe can't seem to understand that God's spiritual domain is far grander than we are able to comprehend and experience. As Paul noted in 1 Corinthians 15:19, the difficulties we face in our material world are as nothing compared to our future with God, and all our problems in the here and now contribute to the betterment of our souls. Beyond our lacking a dimension or so enjoyed in the spiritual domain, we are forced to conform to the limiting influence of the material world's physical laws. Scripture suggests that the spiritual world, possessing what seem to be features common to quantum mechanics but on a macro scale, is not limited to those same laws.

I commented to my relative that he went beyond the question I posed in *Family of God,* as instead of asking why bad things happen to people he asked why bad things happen to *good* people. The answer to that, I said, is that he needs to read the Gospel. As every Christian is aware, none of us is truly good. According to Isaiah's comment in Is 64:6, our righteous God's standards, all of our "good" works are like filthy rags. Next to God's selfless nobility, we're stuck in the slime of self-interest, rendering us unable to storm the gates of heaven on our own merit. We must look to the cross rather than to ourselves for our reconciliation with God. Hordes of the unfortunate lost, having not bothered to read the Bible, have succumbed to the devil's lie about what Christianity is, misunderstanding Christianity to be conducting a basically "good" lifestyle. There is no attitude more in opposition to what it means to be a Christian. With that mockery of the cross, Jesus and what He did on the cross for our sakes is unnecessary to them, in the face of Jesus' own claim in John 14:6 that nobody comes to God except through Him. In their ignorance of God they are so comfortable with the general attitude toward self-gratification that they are unable to understand how low their own standards of "goodness" are. History is replete with the collateral damage caused by "good" acts that have involved terrible unintended consequences. The Christian, on the other hand, is humble enough to gladly accept Jesus' painful work on the cross on his behalf.

Paul commented rather frequently in Scripture regarding the false expectation of rewards from God on Earth for their faith, pointing instead for compensation to the future spiritual domain. In 1 Corinthians 15:12-19 for example, he observes that if Christians hope for reward in this world, they are the most miserable of people. Instead, as he noted in Philippians 1:29, Christians are called to respond to Jesus' suffering for our sakes with our own suffering. Although on the surface that sounds like a dismal prospect, the truly Christian life is joyful, endowing the person with peace in the certain knowledge of God's love, strengthened by the Christian's possession of the indwelling Holy Spirit.

The unbeliever knows nothing of this great advantage, and of what he is missing in lacking it. Moreover, Christianity is unique in its possession of a written message from God Himself to mankind through the inspiration upon man by the Holy Spirit in Scripture. Scripture's unique predictive accuracy and consistency identifies it as supernatural in origin. The Word within it carries the authority of our Creator, most fortunately embodying the attributes of love and wisdom that are lacking in the numerous gods that man has created for himself.

One of my favorite insights into the nature of God can be expressed as the action of the indwelling Holy Spirit to comfort the believer as would a mother, to reconcile the loving nature of God with the suffering that must be faced to strip off the selfishness, endowing the believer with the capability for returning God's love toward him.

PART FOUR

A CALL TO SHARE

CHAPTER THIRTEEN

Sharing the Event With Others

For a good twenty years after the event I refused to discuss it with all but my wife and closest family members. I don't like to admit it, but I suppose that a large part of this reluctance to share it with others stemmed from the rudeness of the official at the Oregon highway patrol with whom I had spoken right after it had happened. Nobody likes to think of himself as one of society's fringe elements, and the topic of UFOs definitely qualifies as being out there.

I was tempted once to let it all out during a bike trip with my wife on the way to Williamsburg, Virginia. Our journey was a roundabout one that took us through Roswell, New Mexico, which, of course, is famous for claims of a nearby UFO crash landing. In the middle of the business district of Roswell is an old movie theater that has been converted into a UFO museum of sorts, complete with a gift shop that sold gaudy T-shirts and other UFO memorabilia. The museum also offered paper and envelopes for people to write down their own experiences and send them on to one of the more popular organizations. I grabbed a sheet and began to write my experiences down, but then I looked up from my efforts and glanced at the colorful exhibits. I stuffed the letter in my pocket and we left. It was just too, well, let me just say this: by that time I'd come to appreciate the probability that the encounter I'd had involved God. If that indeed was the case, God deserved better than a garish T-shirt depicting a bug-eyed grey.

By 2004 I had completed my book *Family of God* in which, among other items, I had presented one collateral aspect of the event, the development of an understanding of Jesus' feeding of the multitudes that was consistent with the numerical values presented in the Gospels. This information is noted in Part Five below. But I had avoided in that book any mention of anything having to do with Danny. The reason for that reluctance to share was the notion that to do so would be to aggrandize myself with a story of which I was almost too proud. *God alone knows about it*, I thought, *and that is more than sufficient.*

At least seven more years went by after the publication of *Family of God*, and well over two decades after my experiences with Danny, before God set me straight rather sternly about my attitude of maintaining a rigid silence about that aspect of the event. *You have no call for glorifying yourself over the experience with Danny. It was all My doing, if you'll recall. It was Me who placed you in touch with Danny and gave you the compassion to bond with him. It was Me who put you into your wings, and it was Me who gave you the guts to do the flying with Danny, so if there's any glorifying to be had, it's to be Me who gets it. I want people to know how faith in Me can change their lives. Get your Bible out and read the Parable of the Talents.*

I did so. Matthew 25:14-30 describes a man who, before taking a long trip, gives his property to three men to invest for him while he is gone. He gives one five coins, to another two coins, and to a third one coin. The men who had received the five and two coins put them to use by investing them. The third man hid his single coin, attempting to keep it safe from loss. When the traveler returned, the men who had invested his money doubled what they were given, and they gave everything back to the traveler. But the third man simply dug his coin up and gave it to the man who had asked him to invest it.

The traveler praised the two for their wise investments, but he was angry with the third man, who gave him back nothing but the original coin. Rather than inviting him to participate in the joy of the Lord like he did the others, the traveler called this man wicked and slothful. He ordered the man to give his single coin to the man to whom he had given the five coins. In this obvious allusion to the propagation of the Gospel, His great commission to us, Jesus concluded with this remark:

> "For every one that hath shall be given, and he shall have abundance; but from him that hath not shall be taken away even that which he hath. And cast the unprofitable servant into outer darkness; there shall be weeping and gnashing of teeth."

I think you can imagine how quickly that passage got me off my rear end and into the writing of *Buddy*, a novel that fictionalized my adventures with Danny. I recounted those adventures later in my nonfiction book *Marching to a Worthy Drummer.*

The cover of *Buddy* has interesting roots. As I had noted earlier, on my first jump off the cliff with Danny, a lady wuffo, unbeknown to me, had taken a photo of the event, a copy of which she later gave to me. I gave it to my brother, who had it enlarged and gave it back. That's the picture on the cover of *Buddy.* I'm in the black helmet and Danny's in the red one. At the upper right is Harold, who's tethered to a stump with a rope around his waist. Harold's courage is legendary; he was absolutely necessary in bringing the event to fruit. (In hang gliding parlance, a wuffo is an onlooker. The term comes from the pumpkin-patch expression "wuffo you do that?" that some wuffos have been heard to mouth.)

In between *Buddy* and *Marching,* I expanded on *Buddy* with three more novels in the *Buddy* series, *Cathy, Jacob* and *Home, Sweet Heaven.* I had become so fascinated with the fictional characters Earl and Joyce Cook that I wanted to see what would become of them! But far more importantly, God had shown me a way, through those novels, to impart some of the knowledge that He had given me, so that the stories would be Scripturally informative as well as entertaining.

CHAPTER FOURTEEN

Facing Critics

An important motivating factor for my first book *Family of God* was to put in print the results of my investigation into Jesus' feedings of the multitudes. But that wasn't the primary driver. Of greater importance was the follow-up to my vision of the Holy Spirit. For several years after that vision I "went with the flow" of mainstream theology which thought of the Holy Spirit either in masculine or genderless terms. Apparently the Holy Spirit took a dim view of my attempt to suppress Her feminine gender, as She prodded me to investigate the gender matter through Scripture and studies performed by theologians. After doing some research and pondering the purpose of a Trinitarian Godhead, I addressed the issue of the Holy Spirit's femininity somewhat tentatively in Part One of *Family of God*. That essay was the result of my first speculative investigation into the possibility that the Holy Spirit did indeed possess a feminine functional nature.

After giving a copy of *Family of God* to a friend who possesses a doctorate in theology, I was both surprised and left bereft by his negative response. He told me directly that my concept of the Holy Spirit was "untenable", and explained the reasons why he felt that way. After his discussion with me, I was tempted to return to the mainstream flow of understanding. But I felt like I had lost a treasured companion. Despite my disappointment in his assessment I appreciated his forthrightness, for after a short hiatus in my pursuit of the truth, his own notion of God gave me a basis for further investigation of Scripture regarding the issue. As it turned out, that follow-on investigation developed in me an even stronger conviction regarding the Holy Spirit's femininity.

Armed with enough information to rebut my friend's challenges, I included it in my first novel *Buddy*. While Danny's adventures in the air provided the organizing topic for *Buddy*, the novel also was a means of furnishing insights into Scripture. Having established a solid logical foundation for the feminine nature of the Holy Spirit, I was highly motivated to include this Scripturally-based insight in the book. Having taken a cue from the Book of Proverbs, wherein Wisdom is presented in a feminine persona, I gave the same name to the Holy Spirit who interacted so intimately with my character Earl Cook.

In the latter half of *Buddy*, Earl Cook experiences confrontations with two pastors. One of them displays a rather benign indifference to the topic of a gendered Holy Spirit, in effect holding to the opinion that while he doesn't agree with Earl's conviction, he does not consider Earl's position on the topic to be of sufficient variance from basic Christian dogma as to exclude him from the Christian community. The other pastor takes a much harsher stance, to the extent that his whistleblowing attempts jeopardize Earl's job and his standing within the community and the Christian Church. The two pastors in *Buddy* reflect the shifting states of my theological friend's responses to my rather tentative treatment in *Family of God* of the Holy Spirit and his comments regarding His attitude regarding my understanding of the Holy Spirit resides somewhere between these two extremes, moving at times between a desire for disciplinary firmness and reserved acceptance. I'm still waiting for him to take a whole-hearted stand for one position or the other. Much of the debate presented in *Buddy* reflects our own discussions, and I'm grateful to him for so ably informing me of the historic and currently prevailing viewpoints of the clergy on the topic. Much of the Church laity has little access to these insights, as the subject is rarely discussed among the great unwashed masses. I think what astonishes me the most about these viewpoints is an apparently very popular one that the Godhead is entirely genderless, which would make God equivalent to an alien being. He might as well be merely the driver of a flying saucer. How are we supposed to love our God with the fervor commanded by Moses and Jesus in the presence of that viewpoint?

At any rate, here I stand, a heretic for all practical purposes. It isn't comfortable, but I'd rather be a heretic than subscribe to some of the silly childish Pablum that pastors have been getting from their seminaries and disseminating to their own congregations.

I am a heretic in more ways than I care to count. To the Church my heresy (in addition to my viewpoint regarding the Holy Spirit) is that I dare to mention God and UFOs in the same sentence. To that fringe group of Christians that perceive some UFOs as demonic, my heresy is that I dare to perceive UFOs in a positive light. To the UFO community, my inexcusable heresy is that I dare to mention God and UFOs in the same sentence. To every conceivable permutation of Christians and UFO buffs, it's considered best, during the time that they discuss either Christianity or UFO phenomena, that I remain in the car.

Jesus was crucified for His apparent heresy, so from that aspect, at least, I guess I'm in excellent company.

Chapter Fifteen

Understanding the Feminine Side of God

After my having included perceptions about the Holy Spirit in my novels, I continued to research the topic of the Holy Spirit's femininity. By this time my understanding of the Holy Spirit had developed to the point where I felt that it would justify a more formal nonfiction follow-up to *Family of God*. The result of that effort is the book *Marching to a Worthy Drummer*. In *Marching*, I offer a detailed justification for considering the Holy Spirit to be functionally feminine. The following discussion summarizes the conclusions that I had reached there regarding that topic.

Some of the points I make below admittedly are of an abductive nature, and therefore suffer from a degree of uncertainty. Abductive logic takes the form of "if event A causes subsequent event B, then if event B has been found to have occurred, event A may have been the cause". This logical route, unlike deductive reasoning, does not firmly identify A as the cause, as if another event C exists, such that C also causes subsequent event B, then event C, rather than A, may have been the cause of B. If event A is the only known cause of B, which is the case with several of the following items, then placing the cause of B on A stands on firmer ground. Also, if there are several events, all of which have occurred and all of which point to prior cause A, then the greater the number of these, the more confidence one can have in A being the actual cause.

Among the items below that associate femininity with the Holy Spirit, some are supporting considerations and others are rebuttals to stated objections. I'll address the supporting elements first.

Spiritual birth: In John 3, Jesus describes the Holy Spirit as giving spiritual birth. Birth is an eminently feminine function.

Scriptural references to femininity: As several qualified scholars have noted, the feminine gender is applied to the Holy Spirit in the original Hebrew Old Testament Scripture and in the original Aramaic and Syriac New Testament Scriptures. These references include Genesis 1:2, numerous instances in Job and Judges, Isaiah 51:9 and 10, John 14:26 (Sinaitic Palimpsest) and Romans 9:25. In the instances cited, the application of feminine descriptors went beyond mere grammatical convention.

The Shekinah Glory: The Shekinah Glory, seen as fire and smoke from God, indwelt the Tabernacle in the Wilderness (Exodus 40) and Solomon's Temple (1 Kings 8) at their dedications. This indwelling was a type of the Holy Spirit's indwelling of the human temples of believers, beginning at the first Pentecost following Jesus' resurrection (1 Corinthians 3:16, 2 Corinthians 6:16 and Ephesians 2:19-22). The Shekinah Glory is grammatically feminine and was seen as feminine in Jewish tradition as well.

The marriage of Christ with His Church: In Ephesians 5:31 and 32, Paul plainly writes that in the spiritual realm, Jesus will marry His Church. His manner of description identifies that marriage as more than a trivial play on words. There and elsewhere, the Church is identified as feminine. If Jesus, a Member of the Trinitarian Godhead, marries the gendered Church, it is likely that the other Members are married as well. This would require that the Holy Spirit be feminine.

The femininity of Wisdom in Proverbs: The gender of Wisdom in Proverbs is consistently feminine throughout. The linkage of Wisdom with creation, particularly in Proverbs 3 and 8, suggests that Wisdom represents the Holy Spirit.

The linkage of Wisdom with the Holy Spirit in the Book of Wisdom: The Book of Wisdom, which remains canonical in the Catholic Scriptures, depicts Wisdom as the Holy Spirit and feminine.

The executive function of the Holy Spirit: The Holy Spirit is described in Scripture in the role of executive to the Father. This responsive role to the Father's will is feminine in nature.

The creation of Adam and the formation of Eve are suggestive of the femininity of the Holy Spirit: The creation of mankind as gender-differentiated in the image of God (Genesis 1:26 and 27) is suggestive of the gendered nature of the Godhead and consequent femininity of the Holy Spirit; the follow on description of the formation of Eve out of Adam (Genesis 2:18-25) probably is a repetition for the sake of emphasis instead of its usual awkward and confusing interpretation as a redundant secondary creation account. The account may well be a type of events within the Godhead Itself.

The romantic nature of the Song of Solomon: The Song of Solomon, considered by many Bible commentators to be representative of the romantic and passionate nature of the marriage between Christ and His Church, depicts the Church as feminine. The romance in Songs must typify either the relationship between Christ and His Church, or between the Father and the Holy Spirit, or both; otherwise it wouldn't belong in the Bible. The same comment made with regard to the marriage between Christ and His Church in Ephesians 5 applies here: if one Member of the Godhead marries, it is suggestive that marriage applies to all within the Godhead.

Monotheism vs. the Trinitarian Godhead: Christianity is a firmly monotheistic religion. In the face of this, it also acknowledges a Trinitarian Godhead. Only in the context of marriage and family can the declared oneness of God (Deuteronomy 6:4) be intuitively reconciled with a Trinitarian Godhead. I personally have been exposed to admissions of confusion by multiple theologians who, while not accepting the family nature of the Godhead, remain oblivious to the important paradox that results from their view.

Biblical proscriptions against sexual deviation: In the context of a genderless or all-male Godhead, the proscriptions against the variety of sexual lifestyles indulged in by modern society, such as those in Leviticus 18 and 20 and Romans 1, appear to be arbitrary; in the context of a gendered masculine and feminine Godhead, on the other hand, any sexual activity other than that within a one woman, one man marital relationship would represent a violation of the type of the Trinity Itself. Perhaps the most serious of these deviations, according to that understanding, would be participation in adultery.

In addition to the considerations made above that directly support a feminine Holy Spirit, appeals can be made in rebuttal to frequently-made objections to the Holy Spirit's femininity. In contrast with the supporting features noted above, all of the objections here may be stated abductively, where the objections are stated in the form of prior causes C to results D that point to a non-feminine Holy Spirit. Consequently, all of the objections admit of rebuttals, where the rebuttals then may be stated as alternate prior causes A for which result D points to a feminine Holy Spirit. These considerations are described below.

The "He" issue: The Holy Spirit is referenced by masculine pronouns in multiple locations of Scripture, e.g. John 14:16, 14:26, 15:26, 16:7 and 8 and 13-15, and Hebrews 3:7 and 10:15, although some verses reference the Holy Spirit in neuter terms. These references constitute the most common argument against a feminine Holy Spirit.

There are at least two alternate reasons for this use of masculine pronouns that permit the Holy Spirit to be viewed as feminine. The first is the distinction between substance and function, which invokes the notion that the Holy Spirit, being linked by substance to the Father, may be male in substance, whereas She is female with regard to Her functional nature. The second, and most likely, alternative is that the translations of Scripture that are available to us don't accurately follow the original in gender assignment.

With regard to the second alternative, we know that the Hebrew name of Spirit, *ruah,* is feminine, while the Greek equivalent, is neuter and the Latin equivalent is masculine. These language-based gender differences may partially account for the gender switch in the translations. The more likely scenario, unpleasant as it may be to consider, is that the switch was deliberate. The Jewish religion had, for the most part, viewed the Holy Spirit as feminine, as did a large group of early Christians, as demonstrated by the femininity of the Holy Spirit in the Syriac Scriptures. In addition, the Siniatic Palimpsest, the original writing of which is thought to be close or identical to the Gospel that Paul taught from, depicts Jesus in John 14:26 as describing the Holy Spirit as feminine. There are multiple reasons why it is thought that the switch was deliberate: first, the neuter description of the Arm of the Lord in Isaiah 51:9 and 10 is known to be a deliberate switch from the feminine; second, the prevailing sexual debauchery of the secular society surrounding the Christian community led the Christian leaders to set the Church aside in perfect purity, even to the extent that motivated some early Christian males to attempt to castrate themselves. Sometimes, as was possibly the case with Origen (according to Eusebius), the attempt was successful. Many of the early Church Fathers, including Justin Martyr, Clement of Alexandria, Tertullian, Origen, Ambrose of Milan, and, most famously, Augustine, vehemently equated purity with chastity. Some of them were misogynistic as well. A third reason that I see for the switch is the pressure of numerous heresies that confronted the early Church. One important threatening heresy was Gnosticism, which favored a femininity of the Holy Spirit. The switch to the masculinity of the Holy Spirit was probably complete around the time of Constantine.

Scriptural references to gender neutrality: Two such references stand out in particular: Galatians 3:28, which declares that in the spiritual realm humans are neither male nor female, and Matthew 22:30, in which Jesus asserts that in the resurrection, men and women neither marry nor are given in marriage. These passages are frequently interpreted as declaring that the realm of God in heaven is genderless. Note also that Jesus in Matthew 22, while describing individuals as not marrying in the spiritual domain, also associates that situation with the power of God, which seems inappropriate in the context of God lacking the gender attribute that we enjoy so thoroughly. This association would be far more appropriate for gender in a grander sense, as with the Church as a collective as well as within the Godhead itself.

The obvious alternative interpretation, which also is a more logical one, is that while individual humans aren't gendered in the spiritual realm, their aggregate, as the Church, is indeed gendered, that gender being female. Paul himself, in describing spiritual gifts in 1 Corinthians 12, depicts spiritual humans as components of the church, likening them to body parts such as ears. Body parts of themselves are not gendered. In the material realm, the exercise of gender requires a multitude of body parts, including the mind, interacting in close cooperation. Scripture indicates that this is precisely how gender works in the spiritual realm. That being the likely case, the Scriptural references noted above make no statement whatsoever about a supposed lack of gender in the spiritual realm.

Wisdom associated with the Holy Father as a personal attribute: To those who consider the Godhead to be either masculine or genderless, their bond is seen in somewhat similar terms to that which may be found in a corporate boardroom. In that context, in Jeremiah 10:12, where God describes His creation as being made by His power and wisdom, those descriptors are naturally interpreted as His personal attributes.

But there is an alternate interpretation that not only makes more logical sense, but is beautifully descriptive. In that alternate interpretation, the Father and Holy Spirit are considered to be a tightly-bonded couple, each possessing the other in a romantic relationship. Under that alternate understanding, the Holy Spirit, along with Her attributes of Wisdom and Power, are naturally seen as an intimately-loved possession of the Father, and therefore belong to Him as part of Him in the same context as Adam's description of two joining to become one.

The personification of Wisdom in Proverbs is often interpreted as simply a literary device: Those who would deny the femininity of the Holy Spirit correspondingly deny the Personhood of Wisdom. Instead, they view the feminine voice of Wisdom in Proverbs as a literary embellishment of the wisdom of God.

In an alternate and more reasonable interpretation in opposition to the interpretation of wisdom as an impersonal attribute, Jesus Himself, in Luke 7:35, confers motherhood on Wisdom. Motherhood is an eminently personal attribute, was well as being a hallmark of femininity. Jesus more emphatically personifies wisdom in Luke 11:49 and 50, having Her speak and perform actions.

Femininity is viewed as inappropriate to Godhood: This slanderous, misogynistic rebuke of womanhood is surprisingly common among theologians. Paul's commentary in 1 Corinthians 14 on the role of women in Church ("it is a shame for women to speak in the church") is often taken as justification for this view.

Given Paul's beautiful description of the future woman, the Church, in Ephesians 5, and his friendship with many women and use of them in Church activities, his probable intent with regard to womanhood conflicts with the interpretation given above. Several alternate interpretations of his statements are all supportive of feminine Godhood.

The first such alternative view, as I had noted in *Marching to a Worthy Drummer*, sees Eve's error in the Garden as a transgression on her proper role as type of the feminine Holy Spirit by failing to limit her responsive role to that of the will of either her husband Adam or to the Holy Father. In that context, Paul's commentary in 1 Corinthians 14 actually supports a feminine Holy Spirit.

In the second alternate view, Paul is seen as having had an issue with the women at Corinth, and that his admonition regarding women were directed only to them and not to womanhood in general. In that context, Paul would not have furnished justification for regarding the feminine as not suitable for Godhood. The actual canonization of these personal views may have been the acts of later, more patriarchal or misogynistic Church authorities.

In the third alternate view, the words regarding women were not spoken by Paul, but represent a counterfeit insertion of another's words into Scripture and attributed unjustly to Paul. There is ample indication for motive for this kind of untruth in the known misogynistic bias among our early Christian Fathers. In that context as well, justification would be lacking for denying Godhood to the feminine gender.

This work consulted very little, if any, Scripture. Given the words in 1 Peter 3 regarding the woman's duty of submission, the first alternative view is the most likely one.

God is above the passion that a gendered Godhead would suggest: This view arose from the attempt to purify the Church of all sexuality. It was supported by Augustine and other Church Fathers and, centuries later was formalized by medieval cleric Jerome Zanchius in his tome on Absolute Predestination.

Scripture itself provides a rich source of alternate viewpoints, all of which endow God with passion, including love, anger and sorrow. Examples include Exodus 32:10, Hosea 1, Matthew 19, 21, 23 and 26, and Luke 24. Jesus' response to the Pharisees in Matthew 19 indicated a familiarity beyond His human form with love and its implications regarding inter-gender relationships. He was fully aware of the passionate nature of the marital bond and went so far as to claim (Matthew 19:6) that the source of the bond was God Himself.

The grammatical "she" in the Hebrew language does not necessarily indicate femininity: There has been much ado made by deniers of femininity in the Godhead about the fact that some objects are given feminine designators when no actual femininity is involved. The situation here is similar to the standard practice in English of calling a genderless object such as a ship "she".

This argument would typically apply to objects, but not to sentient beings such as humans or Members of our Trinitarian God. If indeed the personification of Wisdom in Proverbs did not refer to an actual Person but was simply a literary device, then this argument might apply.

The alternate explanation is identical to the alternate which applies to the argument noted above that the personification of Wisdom in Proverbs is simply a literary device.

The bottom line with respect to the rebuttals is that for every argument of which I am aware that calls into question the femininity of the Holy Spirit there is at least one alternate explanation, often considerably more reasonable than the original argument, that negates the argument itself and supports the notion of a feminine Holy Spirit. Furthermore, where the argument references Scripture, the rebuttal also appeals to Scripture.

As I review these arguments I find myself to be rather indignant with the poor performance of the mainstream Churches in their utter failure to disseminate to their congregations the true nature of God. But that's not the first time that such has happened: the Pharisees did the same regarding the true nature of Jesus, to which Jesus Himself responded with some rather indignant commentaries of His own.

CHAPTER SIXTEEN

Planting More Seeds

In addition to my books, I also started a blog under the name of friendofthefamily.wordpress.com. I have been updating it around twice a week on the average for several years now. My postings cover a range of topics relating to the understandings given me by the Holy Spirit regarding the Christian faith.

All of my books have been presented there as serial installments. But I also interpret information from news sources that I see as particularly relevant to Christianity as God has found fitting to show me. In that endeavor, I am careful to adhere to a very important part of Church dogma, which is that Scripture, being the very Word of God, is inerrant in the original and inspired by the Holy Spirit as expressly stated by both Paul and Peter.

Paul's version is in 2 Timothy 3:16 and 17:

> *"All scripture is given by inspiration of God, and is profitable for doctrine, for reproof, for correction, for instruction in righteousness. That the man of God may be perfect, thoroughly furnished unto all good works."*

Peter put it this way in 2 Peter 1:20 and 21:

> *"Knowing this first, that no prophecy of the scripture is of any private interpretation. For the prophecy came not at old times by the will of man, but holy men of God spoke as they were moved by the Holy Spirit."*

As a practical matter, this means that God, rather than giving me interpretations of Scripture, highlights to my awareness passages in Scripture that are relevant to the information which He wishes to pass on. To that end, though, it is extremely important to recognize that the inspired version of Scripture is the original autograph in the original language and not one of the numerous translations and language interpretations. There is ample evidence that Scripture has been manipulated and tampered with to serve the biases of various Church committees. Bible versions must be chosen with care. The version I prefer is the King James for its colorful expressions, but I'm also careful to be critical of the numerous passages in that version that have been deliberately tweaked.

I summarized the understanding given to me of the Holy Spirit's femininity in a posting entitled "Significance of a Feminine Holy Spirit" on my blog friendofthefamily.wordpress.com. I offer it below to the interested reader:

SIGNIFICANCE OF A FEMININE HOLY SPIRIT

A major implication of perceiving the Holy Spirit's femininity is the replacement of confusion with understanding. Once that connection is made, the Godhead's attribute of Unity in the face of Trinity is no longer a logical inconsistency; the understanding itself immediately emerges with the depth of full intuition, so boldly as to evoke not only a sense of functional differentiation among the Members of the Godhead, but also to resolve the former paradox of unity in Trinity and to encourage the assignment of specific functions to each of them.

The Trinity, given the inclusion of femininity, at once is seen in a Family context. Viewing the Godhead in context of Family, the Family Entity resides above the three Members of the Trinity, representing the oneness of God in loving relationship, to which the individual Members are subordinate. In that setting, the Trinitarian Godhead represents the unity of Family, whereas the individual Members of the Godhead represent the three familiar functional roles of Father, Mother and Son.

In the context of function, the Father naturally represents the Divine Will in accordance with that assignment as given in Scripture, whereas the Holy Spirit responds to that Will by furnishing the Means by which it may be actualized. Pursuing that context, the Son represents the result of the union between Will and Means, being the Will's actuality in Creation.

Key to understanding the Divine Family is the notion of complementary otherness implicit in the relationship. The importance of complementary otherness is its very partiality, which in the incompleteness of one partner without the other removes the exaltation of the individual. Even, or perhaps especially in the Godhead, ego is deliberately minimized by design.

It is my conviction that the Father Himself, in his own selfless nobility, willed the implementation of His subordination to Family, with love as His motive for doing so. Parting Himself in two, He voluntarily limited His unrivaled personal sovereignty over the universe to a shared arrangement with that element of His former essence that we call the Holy Spirit. This parting created gender differentiation within the Godhead Itself As the Complementary Other to the masculine initiative essence of the Divine Father, the Holy Spirit necessarily possesses the responsive gender attribute of femininity.

This Family-based gendered view of the Godhead elevates several verses of Genesis 1 and 2 beyond mere descriptive images of mankind, as we are used to understanding them, to very elemental depictions of the Godhead Itself.

Genesis 1:26 and 27 explains God's desire to make mankind in His own image. The way it was expressed was that this image of God consisted of a plurality of persons, and included both masculinity and femininity as significant features.

In their usual interpretation of this passage, commentators on Genesis regularly interpret the image of God in which man was created to consist of character attributes, avoiding any association of mankind's rather significant gender attributes with God Himself. That interpretation deliberately and without justification ignores the conspicuous inclusion of gender in the passage.

In Genesis 2:18 through 22 the creation of Eve out of Adam is related in interesting detail. As this passage follows the creation of Adam out of the earth and some subsequent activities of Adam, its usual interpretation is that Eve's creation historically followed that of Adam's, without further elaboration. While the sequence under that interpretation may or may not be correct, an interpretation under the understanding of a fully-gendered Godhead is far more significant. The passage begins with God bringing to Adam all the living creatures that He had created and asking him to name them. Then God put Adam to sleep and extracted one of his ribs, from which he formed the feminine Eve, which he brought to Adam.

Under the standard interpretation there are some enigmatic elements, such as the question as to why God had Adam name the beasts before giving him Eve, and why God didn't prescribe the same procedure for creating female animals out of the males.

The answer is, obviously, that man alone out of Creation was made in God's image, and the account of the creation of Adam and Eve in God's image says something about God Himself as well as mankind. The passage quoted above is not incidental; it is an elaboration for emphasis of God's own nature.

Note in that passage that God described the state of Adam being without a companion as not good. Being without a feminine companion would render Adam, for all practical purposes, genderless. The attribute of gender was important to God, which suggests that God considers gender and its exercise as intrinsically good, rather than bad. The passage goes out of its way to make that plain. Again, in an interpretation more in line with what the Scripture suggests, the formation of Eve from Adam echoes rather distinctly the Father's extraction of the Holy Spirit from His own essence.

Directly following that passage in Genesis 2:23-25 is another gender-oriented one:

> "And Adam said, This is now bone of my bones, and flesh of my flesh; she shall be called Woman, because she was taken out of Man. Therefore shall a man leave his father and his mother, and shall cleave unto his wife; and they shall be one flesh. And they were both naked, the man and his wife, and were not ashamed."

Adam spoke these words before the Fall; therefore the union between man and woman was viewed by the primal couple as being God-given and nothing to be ashamed of, precisely as God intended. It was only after the Fall that sexual shame came into the picture.

This passage was so important to God that it was repeated twice elsewhere in Scripture, first by Jesus in Matthew 19:4 through 6 and then by Paul in Ephesians 5:31 and 32.

In Matthew 19 Jesus also repeats Adam's statement regarding Adam and Eve's gender-based relationship, but attributes the act to God Himself, concluding that what God had put together, no man should separate.

In the passage in Ephesians, Paul repeats the event of God having made man in male and female versions for the purpose of the man's leaving father and mother and cleaving to his wife to become one flesh. Then he makes the starkly momentous statement that he's really talking about the relationship between Jesus and His Church.

Adam's quote is obviously important to God, not only because it was echoed by Jesus and Paul, but makes the claim that Jesus, as a Member of the Godhead, will marry the Church. The implication in this is that if gender union applies to one of its Members, it places the attribute of gender squarely in the Godhead, suggesting that gender is an attribute shared by the Father and Holy Spirit as well. Moreover, gender appeals to our intuition, making sense of the relationships within the Godhead. It is easy to picture the fruit of the union between Father and Holy Spirit being the Son Jesus, the glorious actualization of the Will as given birth by the Divine Means.

Here's the great beauty of what the Father did in his selfless parting of Himself to form the Holy Spirit: what He gave up in doing that He regained in love in union with Her. *That* is the true significance of the implication of Adams words: "a Man shall cleave unto to his Wife, and they two shall be one Spirit."

Just as Adam's side was rent to form Eve, and as the Church was formed out of Jesus' pierced side on the cross, so did the Father part Himself to form the Holy Spirit, with Whom He united in love to form Jesus Christ.

God intended our relationship with Him to be intimate and romantic. Only through our perception of the Godhead in Family terms can we begin to appreciate and love God as Jesus calls us to do in Matthew 22:37 and 38:

> ". . .Thou shalt love the Lord, thy God, with all thy heart, and with all they soul, and with all thy mind. This is the first and great commandment."

CHAPTER SEVENTEEN

How the Church Got Where She Is

Having become convinced of the Holy Spirit's feminine gender but frustrated at the indifference of my Christian friends and the Church in general over a period of almost two millennia toward what to me was an earth-shaking revelation, I realized that if this understanding was to be credible, there would have to be a convincing picture of how the Church could have been so misled. After a period of three more years' research toward the objective of tying in motives together with a probable sequence of events that led up to the misrepresentation of the Holy Spirit as male, I have come up with the following narrative. To me, it rings true; perhaps the reader will agree that it's a reasonable account.

By the time of the Protestant Reformation in the sixteenth century, Church doctrine had been thoroughly established: the Nicene, Apostles' and Athanasian creeds had been fully accepted by mainstream Christianity, and, for the most part, elevated to the status of Scripture, which they supposedly represented in summary form. Out of this rigidly-held doctrine, the Trinity was perceived as one God with three distinct personalities, co-equal and co-existent throughout eternity. Although all three Persons of the Godhead were assigned the masculine gender, the gender itself was treated as nonsexual: the Persons were assigned secondary masculine attributes, those associated with character and personality, but the primary reproductive attribute of sexuality was almost universally considered to be beneath the nature of God. Medieval cleric Jerome Zanchius, a contemporary of Martin Luther's and highly-respected as a valid Christian theologian and spokesman of the faith, carried this notion to the extreme of denying God passion as well.

It is not difficult, given the background and mindset of early Christians, to acquire a likely scenario as to how this state of affairs came to be. As part of this process, the Holy Spirit had suffered a switch in gender long before the Reformation, at about the time that the Church herself enjoyed a switch in status in the fourth century from persecution to acceptance.

Paul, in support of the Christian desire for moral cleanliness and writing to a persecuted Church that was ever in danger of returning to the materialism of society at large, added his obviously conflicted opinion of the meaning of sexual purity and the role of women within the Christian economy, but questioning himself as he did so as to whether he was writing on behalf of the Holy Spirit, or whether his was doing so entirely on his own. In 1 Corinthians 7:1 and 2, 25-40, he embellished on Jesus' suggestion in Matthew 19 that some men would be made eunuchs for the sake of a whole-hearted devotion to God, attempting to apply this notion to mankind in general:

> "Now concerning the things about which ye wrote unto me, it is good for a man not to touch a woman. Nevertheless, to avoid fornication, let every man have his own wife, and let every woman have her own husband. . . .

> "Now concerning virgins, I have no commandment of the Lord; yet I give my judgment, as one that hath obtained mercy of the Lord to be faithful. I suppose, therefore, that this is good for the present distress, I say, that it is good for a man so to be. Art thou bound unto a wife? Seek not to be loosed. Art thou loosed from a wife? Seek not a wife. But and if thou marry, thou hast not sinned; and if a virgin marry, she hath not sinned. Nevertheless, such shall have trouble in the flesh; but I spare you. But this I say, brethren, The time is short; it remaineth that both they that have wives be as though they had none; and they that weep, as though they wept not; and they that rejoice, as though they rejoiced not; and they that buy, as though they possessed not; and they that use this world, as not abusing it; for the fashion of this world passeth away. But I would not have you without care. He that is unmarried careth for the things that belong to the Lord, how he may please the Lord; but he that is married careth for the things that are of the world, how he may please his wife. There is a difference also between a wife and a virgin. The unmarried woman careth for the things of the Lord, that she may be holy both in body and in spirit; but she that is married careth for the things of the world, how she may please her husband. And this I speak for your

own profit; not that I may cast a snare upon you, but for that which is comely, and that ye may attend upon the Lord without distraction. But if any man think that he behaveth himself uncomely toward his virgin, if she pass the flower of her age, and need so require, let him do what he will, he sinneth not; let them marry. Nevertheless, he that standeth steadfast in his heart, having no necessity, but hath power over his own will, and hath so decreed in his heart that he will keep his virgin, doeth well. So, then, he that giveth her in marriage doeth well; but he that giveth her not in marriage doeth better. The wife is bound by the law as long as her husband liveth; but if her husband be dead, she is at liberty to be married to whom she will, only in the Lord. But she is happier if she so abide, after my judgment; and I think also that I have the Spirit of God."

From the very birth of Christianity at the first Pentecost following Jesus' resurrection, the new Church, either anticipating or echoing Paul's sentiments. swept away from the Christian faith the decadent and often lewd practices associated with the worship of the pagan gods. Gone was the old leaven, and, like a breath of fresh air, the Holy Spirit came to indwell, ennoble and thoroughly clean human temples. With the new faith came an urgent call to demonstrate its difference from the crassness and moral filth of the surrounding secular society. This desire to create a distance between Christianity and the secular/pagan community was expressed, for example, by Justin Martyr, whose writings included his obvious interpretation of Paul's discussion of marriage as being a hindrance to the worship of God. In his writings, which were influential within the Christian community, one can see the beginning of the popular notion among Christians that chastity and purity are two sides of the same coin.

Although Paul repeatedly noted that the union between man and wife is not sinful, it was his admonition that life as a eunuch was better, in that it permitted undiluted focus to the Lord. It was that sentiment which stood out in the early Christian mind as the golden standard of behavior.

Justin Martyr reinforced that standard in his first apology for (defense of) Christianity, as compiled in the book *Early Christian Fathers*, edited by Cyril C. Richardson. This commentary was written around the middle of the second century A.D., about a half century after the Apostle John wrote the Book of Revelation. In it, Justin echoed the sentiment of Paul regarding sexual circumspection:

"About continence [Jesus] said this: 'Whoever looks on a woman to lust after her has already committed adultery in his heart before God.' And: 'If your right eye offends you, cut it out; it is better for you to enter into the kingdom of Heaven with one eye than with two to be sent into eternal fire.' And: 'Whoever marries a woman who has been put away from another man commits adultery.' And: 'There are some who were made eunuchs by men, and some who were born eunuchs, and some who have made themselves eunuchs for the Kingdom of Heaven's sake; only not all [are able to] receive this.

"And so those who make second marriages according to human law are sinners in the sight of our Teacher, and those who look on a woman to lust after her. For he condemns not only the man who commits the act of adultery, but the man who desires to commit adultery, since not only our actions but our thoughts are manifest to God. Many men and women now in their sixties and seventies who have been disciples of Christ from childhood have preserved their purity; and I am proud that I could point to such people in every nation. . . But to begin with, we do not marry except in order to bring up children, or else, renouncing marriage, we live in perfect continence. To show you that promiscuous intercourse is not among our mysteries – just recently one of us submitted a petition to the Prefect Felix in Alexandria, asking that a physician be allowed to make him a eunuch, for the physicians there said they were not allowed to do this without the permission of the Prefect. When Felix would by no means agree to endorse [the petition], the young man remained single, satisfied with [the approval of] his own conscience and that of his fellow believers."

In writing about the sexual purity of Christians, Justin intended to contrast this behavior with that associated with the false gods and the rampant and often cruel immorality that not only was involved in the worship of them, but which had infected secular life as well. He overlooked the fact that God Himself had made man male and female with the intent that this attribute be exercised, but it seems that he, like Paul, thought the end of the age was close at hand and that the material world and all within it would be shortly passing away, making it imperative that all focus should be on things spiritual.

The Church eventually trespassed beyond the bounds of loving worship, propriety and common sense in her effort to cleanse herself, even to the extent of corrupting Scripture. But that took more time, on the order of several hundred years.

Two and a half centuries after Justin, Augustine experienced much the same revulsion over the moral tawdriness of the Roman society in which he lived. Having become a Christian thirty two years after his birth in 354 A.D., Augustine had spent much of his dissolute pre-Christian years in the enjoyment of the depravity of the society in which he lived. The shame and regret of these early years served to drive Augustine into a passionate rejection of loose morality and unbridled lust. The strength of his feelings in that regard are demonstrated throughout his book *City of God*, an example of which is given in Chapters 4 and 5 of Book II:

"When I was a young man I used to go to sacrilegious shows and entertainments. I watched the antics of madmen; I listened to singing boys; I thoroughly enjoyed the most degrading spectacles put on in honour of gods and goddesses – in honour of the Heavenly Virgin, of Berecynthia, mother of all. On the yearly festival of Berecynthia's purification the lowest kind of actors sang, in front of her litter, songs unfit for the ears of even the mother of one of those mountebanks, to say nothing of the mother of any decent citizen, or of a senator; while as for the Mother of the Gods - ! For there is something in the natural respect we have towards our parents that the extreme of infamy cannot wholly destroy; and certainly those very mountebanks would be ashamed to give a rehearsal performance in their homes, before their mothers, of those disgusting verbal and acted obscenities. Yet they performed them in the presence of the Mother of the Gods before an immense audience of spectators of both sexes. If those spectators were enticed by curiosity to gather in profusion, they ought at least to have dispersed in confusion at the insults to their modesty.

"If these were sacred rites, what is meant by sacrilege? If this is purification, what is meant by pollution? And the name of the ceremony is 'the *fercula*', which might suggest the giving of a dinner-party where the unclean demons could enjoy a feast to their liking. Who could fail to realize what kind of spirits they are which could enjoy such obscenities? Only a man who refused to recognize even the existence of any unclean spirits who deceive men under the title of gods, or one whose life was such that he hoped for the favour and feared the anger of such gods, rather than that of the true God."

Augustine was enormously influential to the Christian Church at a time when Church doctrine was still being formulated and heresies were still emerging, to be debated upon and rejected. In his wake, the Church charted a course that polarized herself away from any hint of the depravities associated with the corrupt gods and goddesses of the world about her. This extremity of purification, for which purity overtly was equated with chasity, cleansed the Judeo-Christian God of any taint of sexuality.

During those early years the Christian community also had to contend with a number of conflicting understandings of the nature of God that arose and caused contentious and divisive issues. Various documents regarding the Gospel and the nature of the Trinitarian God were circulated, sometimes conflicting with each other. These disparate accounts caused

St. Jerome, the creator of the Vulgate translation of Scripture, to complain about the differences and question which of them was the most truthful. That work, completed in 404 A.D. after several interruptions, also was influential in establishing Christian doctrine.

Well prior to that, the differences in documents supported differences in belief that began to separate the Christian community into factions. The Gnostics held fast to their perception in alignment with the common Jewish understanding of the Holy Spirit as possessing a feminine nature and functionality in opposition to the larger Roman community, which increasingly leaned in the direction of a genderless God. This difference reached the emerging New Testament documents of the Rome-based Church which, in the end made a gender switch of the Holy Spirit from feminine to masculine. The authorship of this momentous event is unknown, but it changed the inspired and inerrant original version of what later was canonized in Holy Scripture into something less than inspired or inerrant.

The gender conflict was not universal at the time, and didn't achieve official status until the Council of Nicaea was convened in 325 A.D. by the Emperor Constantine, or perhaps even after that event. The thrust of the council was to address several deviations from the Roman understanding of Scripture that were considered to be heretical. Prominent among these were the Arian and Gnostic heresies.

Arius, focusing on the nature of Jesus Christ as the Son of God, claimed that since He came from God, there was a time when Jesus didn't exist. This follow-on status of Jesus, Arius claimed, meant that He wasn't truly God in the same sense as the Father.

The Gnostics, on the other hand, had peevishly separated from the more mainstream Roman Church over their theological differences. In particular, the Gnostics rejected the emerging Roman Scripture. In going off on their own without benefit of Scripture, they fell prey to a number of odd theories and beliefs, and subsequently lost all credibility with the rest of the Christian community. Of all the commentaries on this descent of the Gnostics into confusion, the highly-entertaining discourse of Irenaeus (130-202 A. D.) in *Against Heresies*, particularly against Marcion and his Aeons, is a classic. Incidentally, Irenaeus also wrote on the connection between Wisdom and the Holy Spirit. Wisdom, of course, is the feminine *persona* in Proverbs.

It was in this setting, particularly in the fourth and early fifth centuries A. D., that the Christian faith itself developed the canon of the New Testament and established its structure and dogma as it confronted those serious heresies that threatened to undermine the character and teachings of Jesus and His Apostles. The canon of Scripture, always directed by the Holy Spirit, remained untouched by the human condition. But the Church and the formulation of her dogma were heavily influenced by the deep antagonism in the minds of the Christian leadership fomented by the clamor of incessant, often heated debate between their perception of God and those of the several contenders.

By the time the Council of Nicaea convened, Arius had a large following. So did the Gnostics. Others within the Church, who considered themselves more mainstream, were turned off about gender in general, considering themselves purer than their secular and pagan counterparts, who had descended into debauchery. In attempting to elevate themselves above that rabble, they equated chastity with purity. And why not? After all, Jesus Himself remained chaste during His time on earth. Confronted with the clamor of the opposing Arian and Gnostic views of God, the leadership of the convention decided to put their feet down and end the constant bickering forthwith by declaring that Jesus was with the Father forever, not having been born or created by him.

They had failed to realize that Jesus didn't marry for the simple reason that He was already betrothed to the Church, and that the femininity of the Holy Spirit was an established understanding during the original compilation of the Old Testament and during the early years of Christianity. Only recently have Christian theologians such as R. P. Nettelhorst and Johannes van Oort arrived at that conclusion through their intensive study of Scriptural documentation. Appendix One presents ten Scriptural reasons why the Holy Spirit must be of the feminine gender. Appendix Two addresses the importance of the correct gender assignment to the Holy Spirit.

Perhaps it was at this time in the early fourth century, while multiple versions of Scripture were contending for the status of general acceptance and the stamp of the Holy Spirit's inspiration, that God was neutered and the Holy Spirit became a weakly masculine Entity in secondary traits of character without a hint of sexuality, a notion that dismissed any notions of gender within the Trinity. There was collateral damage in this scheme: gone was the Family-based understanding of the Trinity, with its gender-associated roles, to be replaced by nothing but intra-Godhead consensus with the attendant confusion of the various roles played by its Members.

It may instead have happened later in the fourth century or in the early fifth century, and instead of resulting from an actual revision, it may have been caused by nothing more than selecting documents in which the revision had already been made. Regardless, at some time around the fifth century the New Testament, which previously had been a collection of disparate documents that sometimes agreed and sometimes disagreed with each other, was made more uniform with the assignment of masculinity to the Holy Spirit. Having dealt with the passions of the attendees and their ill-tempered arguments, the leadership had finally reached the end of the controversies to their satisfaction. Perhaps they may have been heavy-handed in their finality, but at long last they got all that contention out of their hair and now could turn their attention back to their daily living.

Out of the Council of Nicaea came the Nicene Creed, which specified that Jesus Christ was begotten, not made, by the Father and shares the Father's substance or essence. Given the vagueness of the words *begotten* and *made*, to which any number of meanings or non-meanings may be attached, there is nothing in this creed that actually defines the origin of Jesus out of the Father or pins a gender, or gender lack, on any of the Members of the Trinity. But there are hints in it of an attempt to suppress the issue of gender and to minimize any controversy associated with the nature of the Holy Spirit.

By the time that the Church held her next ecumenical meeting, the First Council of Constantinople in 381 A. D., Christianity had just become the official state religion of Rome. During that meeting, the Nicene Creed was altered. The prevailing opinion is that the alteration was rather slight, but there are some troubling aspects of it. In this new version, the origin of Jesus is placed at the beginning of time, and the Holy Spirit is defined more specifically as proceeding from the Father. If one considers the beginning of time as the point at which creation took place, this change is indeed less than momentous. But these new words do represent a nuanced hardening of position, as do the new words regarding the Holy Spirit. Of more concern is The Filioque, which the Western Church added to the revised Nicene Creed by appending the words *and from the Son* to the words *proceeding from the Father* as applied to the Holy Spirit. The Filioque has significant and troubling theological implications, particularly as it negates any possibility of the Trinity representing a divine Family, as was probably originally intended by Scripture and supported by a feminine Holy Spirit. The Filioque, rejected by the Eastern Church, contributed to the rift in the eleventh century between the Western and Eastern Churches labeled *The Great Schism.*

With the passage of years the original contentions and arguments may have become forgotten, along with the reasons behind the definitions of Father, Son and Holy Spirit as they stood. But as ritual set in, the doctrinal positions associated with the Trinity hardened yet further. This hardening process was further supported by the growing status of the Church, which at the higher levels of rank and privilege, attracted men of dubious character who were more interested in reaping the benefits of the state religion than in furthering the union of God and man. As time went on, it is questionable as to how familiar these men at the top were with Scripture, or whether they actually were saved at all.

In the sixth century A. D. the concept of the Trinity had hardened into what became known as the Athanasian Creed, which had become accepted doctrine within the Western Church. By the time of the Reformation, it enjoyed widespread approval by Catholics and some Protestant Churches, most notably Anglicans and Lutherans, who felt that the Nicene Creed had been so vague with respect to the Trinity that it failed to curtail the old heresies of Arianism, Tritheism and Modalism, which continued to crop up with distressing regularity. The intent of this formulation was to more firmly define the Godhead to help rid the Church of those heresies. The Athanasian Creed was not produced by Athanasius; much of the material echoed the Trinitarian theology of Augustine.

In addition to the more detailed presentation of the Trinity, the creed took it upon itself to speak on behalf of God, assessing severe penalties to those whose beliefs didn't match those which were presented in the creed and thus indulging in a form of blackmail to ensure that Church members would march in unthinking lockstep to that particular drum.

Specifically, the Athanasian Creed defined the source of the Father, Son and Holy Spirit as follows: the Father existed as God forever; the Son also coexisted with the Father as fully God, and was begotten by the Father rather than made or created; the Holy Spirit coexisted fully as God with Father and Son as well, and was neither made, created nor begotten, but proceeds from the Father and Son. Note that this arrangement incorporates the Filioque, which was and remains anathema to the Eastern Church. The creed also specifically defined the three Members of the Trinity as not being three Individuals, nor being one Individual with three natures. They were simultaneously one and distinct, coeternal and coequal with none being before or after the other or greater or lesser than the other. The creed ends with this statement, which omits any mention of salvation by faith alone in the death and resurrection of Jesus Christ on behalf of the sinner: "And they that have done good shall go into life everlasting; and they that have done evil, into everlasting fire. This is the catholic faith; which except a man believe truly and firmly, he cannot be saved."

The creed fails as well to recall to the Christian's mind what Jesus considered the greatest commandment of all: to love God with all the heart, and the mind and the soul. Moreover, the words *made, begotten and proceeding* and their differences among each other are basically meaningless, being completely void of any usefully intuitive information. They can mean anything a person or demagogue would wish them to mean. (Actually, the word *begotten*, having been liberally used in Genesis and elsewhere in Scripture, does have a very specific meaning. The meaning involves sexual reproduction. But in the context of a Godhead that is either all-masculine or genderless, sexual reproduction is off the table, forcing the word to be meaningless.) Beyond that, the insistence upon the *coeternal* feature reaches with unjustified arrogance past the ability of man to know or understand, dimensionally restricted as we are, and the concept can be found nowhere in Scripture.

A thousand years after Augustine, the Church's insistence upon purity had not only remained, but had crystallized into a rigid perfectionism, enshrined by the medieval cleric Jerome Zanchius, an inflexible adherent of the heavenly perfection envisioned by Aristotle and Ptolemy. God, according to Zanchius, was the Embodiment of simplicity, perfection, unchangeability and independency of being. These qualities, in turn, implied that God was above some of the defining characteristics of lesser beings such as the human race. Passion is included among these 'lesser' characteristics constituting the human nature that don't belong to God. A brief excerpt from Zanchius' tome *Absolute Predestination* is given below as an example:

> "I.—When love is predicated of God, we do not mean that He is possessed of it as a passion or affection. In us it is such, but if, considered in that sense, it should be ascribed to the Deity, it would be utterly subversive of the simplicity, perfection and independency of His being. Love, therefore, when attributed to Him, signifies—

> "(1) His eternal benevolence, *i.e.,* His everlasting will, purpose and determination to deliver, bless and save His people. Of this, no good works wrought by them are in any sense the cause. Neither are even the merits of Christ Himself to be considered as any way moving or exciting this good will of God to His elect, since the gift of Christ, to be their Mediator and Redeemer, is itself an effect of this free and eternal favour borne to them by God the Father (John 3.16). His love towards them arises merely from "the good pleasure of His own will," without the least regard to anything *ad extra* or out of Himself.

> "(2) The term implies complacency, delight and approbation. With this love God cannot love even His elect as considered

in themselves, because in that view they are guilty, polluted sinners, but they were, from all eternity, objects of it, as they stood united to Christ and partakers of His righteousness.

"(3) Love implies actual beneficence, which, properly speaking, is nothing else than the effect or accomplishment of the other two: those are the cause of this. This actual beneficence respects all blessings, whether of a temporal, spiritual or eternal nature. Temporal good things are indeed indiscriminately bestowed in a greater or less degree on all, whether elect or reprobate, but they are given in a covenant way and as blessings to the elect only, to whom also the other benefits respecting grace and glory are peculiar. And this love of beneficence, no less than that of benevolence and complacency, is absolutely free, and irrespective of any worthiness in man.

"II.—When hatred is ascribed to God, it implies (1) a negation of benevolence, or a resolution not to have mercy on such and such men, nor to endue them with any of those graces which stand connected with eternal life. So, "Esau have I hated" (Rom. 9.), i.e., "I did, from all eternity, determine within Myself not to have mercy on him." The sole cause of which awful negation is not merely the unworthiness of the persons hated, but the sovereignty and freedom of the Divine will. (2) It denotes displeasure and dislike, for sinners who are not interested in Christ cannot but be infinitely displeasing to and loathsome in the sight of eternal purity. (3) It signifies a positive will to punish and destroy the reprobate for their sins, of which will, the infliction of misery upon them hereafter, is but the necessary effect and actual execution."

Although Zanchius' position on passion is an obvious violation of Scripture, it was accepted by the mainstream Church. One can readily see from the example above that a gendered God certainly was off the table in the eyes of the Church, as was a feminine Holy Spirit.

Most damaging of all, despite Jesus' command, the natural and spontaneous love toward a Family-based Trinity remained largely out of the reach of the Churchgoer through the incomprehensibity of her awkward and extrabiblical creedal descriptions of God.

Credit must be given to the Catholic Church for realizing that something important was missing from her understanding of God. The female half of the human population, having no representation in the Trinity, was sitting out in the cold, almost as if women weren't even relevant to God. This lack flew in the face of Jewish tradition, Jesus' respect for women and Paul's mystical promise that the Church was a feminine entity that one day would marry Jesus.

At least some theologians over the centuries must have been thoughtful enough to wish to do something about that deficiency, but by the time of the Reformation, while vestiges of the Grand Inquisition still remained, the prevailing doctrine was so entrenched that they knew that any move they might make to correct the situation would be met by strong and probably violent opposition from those who, in mindless conformity to tradition, considered themselves to be above the reproach of God. Instead, the Catholic Church applied to Mary all of the attributes that belonged to a feminine Holy Spirit, elevating her to the status of *theotokos* (mother of God) and, in residing above other humans, mother of the Church. It was a good start and was better than the Protestant Church's unstated policy of ignoring the issue completely, but wasn't quite honest. Despite the claims of Catholics that Mary is venerated rather than worshiped as God, she stands in the lofty position of having been born sinless, being prayed to as co-redemptrix, and having been assumed into heaven without experiencing the corruption of physical death. Moreover, the Catholic Church complicated the matter and compounded the dishonesty by failing to re-examine its doctrine of equating chastity with purity. Consequently, the Catholic Mary, in direct opposition to Scripture, was presented, along with Joseph, as celibate throughout her entire life on earth.

Consequently, the Church, both Catholic and Protestant, still misses some vital elements of knowledge regarding the Trinity. Because of this lack, she universally fails to possess the intuitive understanding that would lead to the kind of a loving, intimate relationship with God that Jesus commanded in Matthew 22. She places her members into serious jeopardy of persistent disobedience in that matter. The only mitigating factor in that is that their failure to obey is not a conscious defiance of God.

A more reasoned understanding of the trinity leads to the conviction that the Holy Spirit enjoys a fully-gendered feminine nature, and with it a view of the Trinity, both intimate and intuitive, as a Family Entity. This view is supported by Scripture, particularly in Genesis 1:26 and 27, wherein Moses claims that God in the plural created man in His own image, concluding that in that image man was made both male and female. It is astonishing how so many commentators on that passage, blinded by extrabiblical Church creeds and traditions, describe details of character in man that correspond to those in God while ignoring that emphasis on gender. They remained confined to the very tiny intellectual box imposed by the Church, refusing to think outside of it. Many of them proceeded from there to the misunderstand the account in Genesis 2, repeated for emphasis, of Eve's formation out of Adam's side, often perceiving of this account as merely an afterthought. Some even thought of the account as indicating a substantial time interval between Adam's creation and the formation of Eve.

Fortunately, some theologians did recognize that the account of the extraction of Eve's substance from Adam's side was repeated for its importance, foretelling the similar event of the formation of the Church out of Jesus' pierced side. This understanding was supported and embellished upon by Paul's repetition in Ephesians 5:31 and 32 of Adam's statement regarding that event that pointed directly to Jesus' marriage to His Church:

> "This is now bone of my bones, and flesh of my flesh; she shall be called Woman, because she was taken out of Man. Therefore shall a man leave his father and his mother, and shall cleave unto his wife; and they shall be one flesh."

Yet they failed utterly to perceive that this passage not only foretold Jesus' union with His Church, but that it may also have said something very important regarding the nature of the Holy Trinity, having been a reprise of a similar event that occurred before the foundation of the world: the extraction of the Holy Spirit out of the side of the Father, changing His status from All-in-All to that of one Member of a divine Partnership, and diminishing His position but permitting Him to retrieve in love what He lost in the process. If, as John 14:9 claims, *"He that hath seen me hath seen the Father"*, Jesus must faithfully represent the Father in all things, including His sacrificial, noble and selfless nature. Therefore, it is reasonable to expect that the Father would willingly forsake some treasure that he felt to be dear, such as His supreme, undiluted ownership of the universe, for the sake of elevating love over all else. Consequently, it would be logical to suppose that in a loving, selfless and noble move He removed from His own essence His divine Companion the Holy Spirit, forever changing His status from that of one all-inclusive and self-sufficient Member to that of a Holy partnership.

Through that loving union between the Father and His own divine Complement came first the begetting of Jesus as the first Word of God, as told in Genesis 1:1-5 and John 1-5 and 9:

"In the beginning God created the heaven and the earth. And the earth was without form, and void; and darkness was upon the face of the deep. And the Spirit of God moved upon the face of the waters. And God said, Let there be light; and there was light. And God saw the light, that it was good: and God divided the light from the darkness. And God called the light Day, and the darkness he called Night. And the evening and the morning were the first day."

"In the beginning was the Word, and the Word was with God, and the Word was God. The same was in the beginning with God. All thinks were made by him; and without him was not anything made that was made. In him was life; and the life was the light of men. And the light shineth in darkness; and the darkness comprehended it not . . . That was the true Light, which lighteth every man that cometh into the world."

The view described above of the Godhead and its origins departs radically from Church tradition, particularly the Athanasian Creed. Yet it contradicts only the extrabiblical elements of Church doctrine, remaining faithful to Scripture. Actually, it is more self-consistent, intelligible and faithful to Scripture than the Church creeds and traditions.

This lengthy assessment of the cause and stability of Scripture's misguided replacement of the originally inspired feminine nature of the Holy Spirit with a weakly masculine gender was made to the end that one might understand how significant that error has been toward the misinterpretation of Paul's words in 1 Timothy 2:8-15, which is ignored in some Christian circles and foments anger in others. The impact of the error extends beyond Church matters into homes and domestic conduct between husband and wife. The text of 1 Timothy 2:8-15 is given below as an example:

"I will, therefore, that men pray everywhere, lifting up holy hands, without wrath and doubting; in like manner, also, that women adorn themselves in modest apparel, with godly fear and sobriety, not with braided hair, or gold, or pearls, or costly array, but (which becometh women professing godliness) with good works.

"Let the woman learn in silence with all subjection. But I permit not a woman to teach, nor to usurp authority over the man, but to be in silence. For Adam was first formed, then Eve. And Adam was not deceived but the woman, being deceived, was in the transgression.

*Notwithstanding, she shall be saved in childbearing, if they continue
in faith and charity and holiness with sobriety."*

Was Paul a misogynist, as claimed by many modern Christian
women? Given his beautiful presentations in Galatians and Ephesians
of the essentiality of both male and female in the economy of God, and
particularly in his famous mystery in Ephesians 5, that assessment is
highly doubtful. Even more compelling is the belief, shared among many
committed Christians, that this passage was driven by the Holy Spirit, but
in some difficult-to-understand way.

In fact, these words of Paul may well be strikingly supportive of a
feminine Holy Spirit. In that context, a feminine Holy Spirit is perfectly
responsive to the will of the Father in performing works that implement
His loving vision. By contrast Eve, in succumbing to the serpent, failed to
be responsive to the will of God or the will of her husband, and therefore
directly violated her creation in the type of the Holy Spirit. That fallen
nature of Eve has demonstrated itself often and graphically in the pages of
Scripture. A prime example of this is the corruption of Solomon by some
of his foreign wives, who enticed him to follow after strange gods.

Perhaps just as Moses was denied entry into the Promised Land because
in his anger he failed to represent Jesus Christ, mankind has for centuries
been denied a true and beautiful understanding of the family nature of the
Godhead because men, in their fallen natures, fail to represent the Father's
will to their families and women, in their fallen natures, continue to fail
to represent the Holy Spirit's perfect responsiveness to the Father's will.

As it relates to domestic relations between man and wife, the proper
interpretation of the Holy Spirit as possessing the feminine gender leads to
the understanding that Paul's exhortations regarding women was probably
motivated by wishing to describe the proper role to be played by women
in all areas of their lives. This role was to be in conformance to the type
represented by the Ultimate Woman, God the Holy Spirit in Her nature
of faithfully responding to the will of the Father. It was this role alone,
rather than superiority or inferiority or any other judgment of attributes,
that Paul must have been seeking to clarify.

I repeat for emphasis my strong perception that it is role, and role alone,
that differentiates men and women in the sight of God.

PART FIVE

A DEMAND TO UNDERSTAND

Chapter Eighteen

The Adventure Turns Intellectual

Adjusting to a new marriage along with our additional children and a dog added a degree of complexity to our lives that both of us preferred learning about as time moved on. We were content, for the most part, but sometimes we didn't see eye-to-eye and had to learn how to accommodate our differences in background, personality and outlook without turning our new bond into an adversarial relationship. Having each failed once in marriage, we tried harder this time. But our lives were complex and very busy.

On top of that, I was being nudged – no, make that *pushed* – by the Holy Spirit to delve beyond the surface of the Gospel accounts of Jesus' feeding of the multitudes. It was to my benefit, as I was later to see, being not only a confirmation of the amazing, supernatural depth of Scripture, but also showing me the intimacy with which God relates to His people, the human race. As I noted in *Family of God*, it is exceptionally easy to picture Jesus' words in Mark 8 as a mystery. There is something else to the events, something that Jesus seemed to emphasize to His disciples: why were the numbers of starting loaves and the baskets of remainders so clearly stated, particularly when they seemed so counter-intuitive? Once the push into investigate the feedings got me started, this passage intrigued me to the point of demanding an answer.

Why would the Holy Spirit direct my attention to Jesus' feeding events? What was so important about this facet of Jesus' ministry? Most of all, why see in the process a mystery and particularly at this point in time, when, after almost two millennia, Christianity has been so thoroughly established?

The Holy Spirit does what the Holy Father wishes. It's all up to God, not us. Nevertheless, the Bible indeed contains many mysteries, some of which have been openly described by Paul as such. God seems to have planned it that way in order that man would find from a diligent search the truth in the Word of God, and from that truth, come to know and love his God with the fervor of Jesus' Great Commandment in Matthew 22:37 and 38:

> *"Jesus said unto him, Thou shalt love the Lord, thy God, with all thy heart, and with all thy soul, and with all thy mind. This is the first and great commandment."*

As with other things that we treasure the most, the solving of many of the mysteries of God require patience and hard work. God Himself said as much in Proverbs 25:2:

> *"It is the glory of God to conceal a thing, but the honor of kings is to search out a matter."*

Not all mysteries of God are intended to be understood as soon as they are voiced or set down in Scripture. Many mysteries are intended to be revealed at a certain period of history, some perhaps, as suggested in Daniel 12:4, at the end of the age of man's government on earth.

> *"But thou, O Daniel, shut up the words, and seal the book, even to the time of the end; many shall run to and fro, and knowledge shall be increased."*

The numbers involved in Jesus' feeding of the multitudes present an enigma that has eluded a solution for many centuries. Only recently was it found to be amenable to a mathematical solution, suggesting that the solution to the puzzle was intended for our present age. The proof of the mystery is an amazing image, a sign denied to the generation in which Jesus lived on earth, but now available to all to know that the Lord Jesus Christ is indeed the true Messiah sought by the Jews over centuries of hardship and persecution.

In Mark 8, as I noted above, Jesus made a pointed and direct association of faith with understanding as he spoke with His disciples after feeding four thousand people with seven loaves and a few fish. Significantly, just prior to that incident as recorded in Mark He had encountered the Pharisees, who had sought some confirmation from heaven regarding Jesus' credentials.

Jesus responded to that by sighing deeply and asking why this generation is looking for a sign. He then declares that a sign wouldn't be given to it.

As the account in Mark 8 continues, Jesus recalls to His disciples the events in which He fed the multitudes, as if the details represented something of great importance. As the passage unfolds, Jesus left the multitudes and went in a boat with His disciples to the other side. There was only a single loaf of bread on board, as the disciples had forgotten to stock up with more. As they recognized this lack, Jesus warned them about the leaven of the Pharisees. When they took this warning to have a connection with their lack of bread, Jesus corrected them, asking why they didn't understand what He was trying to say and associated their misunderstanding with hardened hearts. Curiously, Jesus then recounted to them the specifics of the feedings. He asked them how many baskets of fragments resulted from he feedings of the five thousand and the four thousand, to which they responded with the numbers twelve and seven, respectively. Jesus responded to those answers with an odd question: *"How is it that ye do not understand?"*

It is tempting, if one is burdened with a load of presuppositions and wishes to breeze through Mark's Gospel in short order, to think of him as lacking in sophistication. He seems to mix numbers inappropriately into the basic message in Chapter 8, and too many details are left unanswered. Why, for example, did Jesus emphasize the numbers associated with the feedings, as if these values were somehow related to their faith? Jesus painstakingly recalls to His disciples the number of individuals fed and the number of remaining baskets, but fails to complete the picture. How many fragments did each basket contain? Of what importance was the number of baskets of leftovers to the event itself, or to the disciples' faith? How can the number of baskets of leftovers have such theological significance that Jesus placed so much emphasis upon it in the recollection of the feeding events to His disciples? Why were 5,000 fed with five loaves, whereas seven loaves were required to feed the 4,000?

What if Mark, as guided by the Holy Spirit and therefore far from being unsophisticated of word, was actually presenting a truth of great depth? In this light, the passage literally pleads for a deeper understanding of the feeding of the people. When Jesus spoke about the specifics of the feedings to His disciples, it was as if he was presenting the future reader with a riddle and commanding him to solve it.

The feeding of the multitudes did indeed contain the rudiments of such a sign as the Pharisees had requested of Jesus. But the completion of its components had to await the Pentecost. The Gospels also had to be written first, in the unique manner in which they presented the elements for later examination. Next, the Gospels had to be integrated into Scripture and thus become available for open review. Finally, a generation had to emerge whose perspective was conditioned to view Scripture beyond that which is immediately apparent.

My probe into the feeding events took ten years to bear fruit in an answer. One initial problem was a missing piece of information demanded by the analysis that led to the astonishing discovery of a feeding event described in the Old Testament. Another item that frustrated me no end and caused me to drop the project for a fairly long period was the pattern for the feeding of the four thousand, which I couldn't make to correspond with the pattern for the feeding of the five thousand. After much effort, and, I'm sure with God's input, I finally thought outside the box, and what resulted was a pattern that *purposely* was different than for the other feeding event. It was this difference that presented such an information-rich answer.

The mathematical details were presented in Appendices 5-1 and 5-2 to Part Five of *Family of God* and are available to the reader by contacting me at perkinsart44@yahoo.com as long as my supply of books lasts. I was quite pleased to find that once the patterns had been mathematically established, a quick visual inspection of them was sufficient to verify that all the numbers in the Gospels and derived in the analysis matched up perfectly. I present the visual verification in Appendix 2 to *Marching to a Worthy Drummer.*

A number of basic assumptions were made in the development and noted in *Family of God.* They will be addressed here as well. One might readily see from the nature of these assumptions and the arguments made for their justification that a symbolic interpretation of the feeding events is on firmer ground than a dogmatic assertion that the feeding took place exactly as the development might imply. Although the development might reflect the nature of the actual events as they took place, one cannot be certain of this on the basis of the information which we have been given. We can be more sure, on the basis of the information which we do have and the manner in which it dovetails together so well, that Scripture intended to provide the reader of the feeding accounts with a symbolic imagery beyond the plain text. This symbolism gives us both a beautiful picture rich with meaning and a demonstration of the unbounded depth of Scripture.

The first assumption made with respect to the analysis is that the feeding may be described as an ordered one, that the assembly of people may be characterized in terms of rectangular arrays having structured rows and columns. This view departs from the historic one in which the people are imagined to have congregated in a haphazard, amorphous fashion. It may be argued that there is no Scriptural justification whatsoever to impose such order on the assemblies. Yet Scripture itself hints of order in noting the commandment to sit down in companies of fifties and hundreds. If indeed the actual assemblies did not assume rectangular appearances, this reference alone is sufficient to justify at least that symbolic appearance to the reader of Scripture.

The second assumption is that a miracle actually took place, but that its occurrence was also an ordered one and simple to understand. The specific nature of this miracle is in the breaking of the bread, which simply mimics the process of the Word's propagation from ear to mouth without loss. After having been blessed by Jesus, the bread returned to wholeness every time it was broken. That's all there is to it. The rest of the process involves the mechanics of the distribution.

In this process, the breaking of the bread quite openly symbolizes Jesus' act on the cross, and its restoration, being of God rather than leaven, speaks of His regenerative power, most profoundly in His resurrection. The miracle itself equates the physical process with the far more important one of feeding the multitudes with the Word of God. The leaven of the Pharisees that Jesus warned His disciples to beware of referred to the distortion of the Word and its consequent corruption as it was propagated by the religious leadership.

The third assumption is that the congregations consisted of precisely the number of people noted in the Scriptural accounts. Indeed, the word 'about' was sometimes used in describing these numbers. Furthermore, there is at least the suggestion that the numbers should be taken as only approximate in the reference to 'besides women and children'. I would suggest, on the other hand, that these references actually support the significance of the numbers as given, directing the reader to consider the 'core' group defined by the numbers to represent some truth of at least symbolic importance.

The fourth assumption is that the baskets of leftovers contain the same number of fragments for both the feeding of the five thousand and the four thousand. It is certainly not a necessity, nor does Scripture specifically note that the remaining fragments were equally distributed among the baskets. As a matter of fact, the descriptions in Scripture of the baskets involved imply that the baskets for the feeding of the five thousand were handbaskets, smaller than the baskets used in collecting the remainders during the feeding of the four thousand.

The original Scripture notes that the baskets used for the feeding of the 5000 was a small handbasket, for which 5 loaves would be appropriate, while the baskets used for collecting the remainder loaves in the feeding of the 4000 was a larger basket. It was for that reason that the pattern analysis, while assuming an equal number of fragments per basket for both of Jesus' feeding events, was careful in attributing the 5 loaves per basket to the menfolk only in each feeding event.

In actuality, there were women and children in addition to the menfolk in both feeding events. According to Mark 7:31 the four thousand were fed near Decapolis on the south shore of the Sea of Galilee, while, according to Luke 9:10, the five thousand were fed near Bethsaida on the north shore, the implication being that the four thousand were mostly Gentile, while the five thousand were primarily Jewish. Further weight is given to this difference by the fact that the seven baskets of the four thousand correspond to the seven representative Churches that Jesus addressed in Revelation 1:20, while the twelve baskets of the five thousand match the twelve tribes of Israel.

The makeup of the audience is relevant to the size of the baskets in that the practice of the Jewish faith is patriarchal in nature, with the menfolk almost exclusively being involved in the ceremonial ritual. Also, the faith was exclusive in another sense, being restricted to Jews. Given the symbolic nature of the feedings, then, the sizes of the baskets, which represented the growth of the faith, were exceedingly important. The Jewish women and children were certainly fed along with the men, but it was the menfolk to whom the Word of God was primarily directed, it being their responsibility to interpret and direct this Word to their womenfolk. This changed radically with the birth of the Church at the Pentecost following Jesus' resurrection. For the first time, women and even children were to be directly involved in the spread of the Christian faith. This difference is borne out in Acts 2:16 - 18, wherein the Christian women as well as the men not only were involved in the gift of the indwelling Holy Spirit, but were expected to actively use that gift. Referring back to the prophet Joel, Peter's quote regarding the pouring out of the Holy Spirit included the indwelling of the Holy Spirit and the participation of daughters and handmaidens in prophetic speech.

The bottom line is that the menfolk of both the four and the five thousand contributed five loaves to each basket. But the women and children of the Gentile four thousand added their share into the baskets of remainders, while only the menfolk of the five thousand contributed to their baskets of remainders.

The fifth assumption is that in addition to the three events where the 100 of 2 Kings 4, and 5,000 and the 4,000 of the Gospel accounts were actually fed with physical bread there was another, strictly symbolic event, as noted in Scripture, where 3,000 were fed with by Peter with the Word of God. This incident taken from the Acts has been integrated into the others to complete the symbolic image. The Scriptural link between bread and the Word is so emphatic in the Gospels that it requires no further explanation. When Jesus, whom John specifically describes as the Word both feeds the multitudes and claims that "I am the Bread of Life" He makes the obvious connection Himself. When, in John 21, Jesus commands Peter to "Feed my sheep", and repeats this command three times, can one fail to see some prophetic significance to His words? When we as Christians partake of the Sacrament in honor of the Incarnate Word, do we not make that link? Perhaps one cannot expect the multitudes who were fed with physical bread to have appreciated the image they were forming, nor to have linked that bread with the Word. But the symbolic picture that is presented herein was not intended for them. It was intended for the reader of New Testament Scripture who came after all of the events which were described at that time.

Scripture, in recounting Jesus' feeding of the multitudes, furnishes information regarding those events that extend quite deeply beyond the surface of the narrative. The mathematical solution to the feeding of the multitudes requires a complex analysis that draws upon different passages of the Bible, both the Old and the New Testaments, and is comprised of different meanings for the word 'feedings.' There are two very distinct definitions for 'feedings' that must be used together to solve the puzzle. One definition of feedings is nourishment found in food. The other definition of feedings is the nourishment found in the Word; one for sustenance of the body, the other for the sustenance of the soul, as Jesus Himself suggested in Matthew 4:4, when He asserted through Scripture to the devil who was tempting Him that man lives not just by bread, but by every word spoken by God.

The physical bread represented only a part of the feeding events. In fact, it wasn't even the most significant part. The bread was only symbolic of a much greater spiritual Bread, the Word of God.

There are several proofs of this. First, there is the spiritual representation of Jesus in John 1:1 and 14 as the Word of God:

> "In the beginning was the Word, and the Word was with God, and the Word was God - - - And the Word became flesh, and dwelt among us".

Jesus, in fact, considered the material world, including physical bread, to be of little value. According to John 18:36a, Jesus asserted that His kingdom was not of this world.

But even before He made that statement, He was more direct in John 6 regarding the relative importance of bread and His Word. Jesus emphatically claimed there that material food not only needs constant replenishment, while His word is of eternal sustenance and far more important. When He was asked how one goes about obtaining this spiritual food, Jesus asserted that He, as the incarnate Word of God sent from the Father, is freely given to believers in Him.

CHAPTER NINETEEN

An Astonishing Message Buried in the Feedings

As was the case with many other acts that Jesus performed, Jesus' feeding of the multitudes was not the first such incident to have occurred. God had permitted the prophet Elisha to prefigure Jesus in the feedings. The account is given in 2 Kings 4, which states that twenty loaves of barley was sufficient not only to feed one hundred men but to furnish leftovers besides. This Old Testament account, in fact, provides the twenty-by-five pattern of the standard company of one hundred. The ten-by-five pattern of the standard company of fifty is simply a length half that size.

In addition to Elisha's feeding event and the two feeding events associated with Jesus, Peter also enacted three symbolic feeding events as Jesus commanded in John 21. The first of these, the feeding of three thousand with the Word of God as described in Acts 2, is included in the analysis as suggested by the manner in which the pattern for the other three feeding events pointed to their integration into a more general and significant pattern.

In all, the analysis presented in Appendix 5-1 (alternatively, the simpler version presented in Appendix 5-2) to *Family of God* covered four feeding cases: case 1 involved Elisha's feeding of one hundred; case 2 pertained to Jesus' feeding of five thousand; case 3 was associated with Jesus' feeding of four thousand, and case 4 involved Peter's feeding of three thousand with the Word of God as noted in Acts 2.

Interestingly, the two cases associated with Jesus involved all twelve disciples: five for the feeding of the five thousand, and seven for the feeding of the four thousand.

There is one feature of the development that is beyond question: the correctness of the math. It was the math that led me to an understanding of the patterns associated with the feeding events, and its correctness is evident in the fact that the patterns generated from the analysis produce, merely by visual inspection, all the relevant numbers associated with the feedings, permitting the investigator to intuitively derive them on his own. Simply by observing the patterns and the associated feeding process, both of which are shown in *Marching to a Worthy Drummer*, one readily can see how five thousand can be fed from five loaves and produce twelve baskets of remainders, while four thousand can be fed from seven loaves and produce seven baskets of remainders.

As the numbers show, the primary objective of the analysis, that of establishing a logical basis for the numbers associated with the feeding events, was satisfied. A unique numerical value of 5 was found for the number of loaves in each basket collected as remainder, and solutions were found that furnished specific arrangements of individuals for each of the feeding cases. These arrangements were compatible with all the values explicitly noted in Scripture. As far as has been determined, this compatibility is unique to the arrangements presented herein. Although this uniqueness has not been proven, i.e. all possible row by column shapes of companies of 50 and 100 have not been exhaustively analyzed, experience suggests that the possibility is remote of obtaining alternate arrangements that simultaneously satisfy the numerical values presented in Scripture. Of most significance is the reconciliation of the initial loaves with the number fed and the remainder baskets (and loaves) for the two cases where these three parameters were spelled out. A further feature established in this analysis is that the process allows the number of loaves to be reconciled with the number of fish.

Moreover, there was a remarkable consistency of unspecified parameters as well as process among the four events. The solutions emerged under the imposition of a number of consistency-driven constraints: the consistency of process; the limitation of company sizes to the two which were overtly mentioned in Scripture; the consistency of company shape (10 x 5 and 20 x 5); the consistency of the distribution of initial (specified) loaves one to a frontmost company by one disciple of Jesus for each such company; the requirement that the company rows and columns align with each other, coupled with the requirement that each column furnish one and only one remainder loaf; and the consistency of the number of remainder loaves per basket.

An interesting aspect of the analysis is that it finds corroboration in the twenty-first chapter of John's Gospel. The total value of the remainder from all four events, under the assumption of the integration of the first event into the second as suggested below, is 155. This number represents the remainder of either bread or fish because the strict pattern-dependency of these numbers requires the remainders in either case to have the same values. When this number is compared with the number of fish described in John 21, the result provides an additional confirmation of this interpretation of the feeding. For if the 153 fish that the disciples caught is added to the apparent two fish that Jesus had on the fire, the total number of fish noted in John 21 is also 155.

There were, however, two exceptions to the general consistency of pattern. The analysis actually produced far more information than anticipated, and this information came out of these exceptions.

The first exception was the orientation parameter u in the analysis, which was not consistent among the cases, differing in Case 3 from the other three. Among the initial assumptions of consistency for the event in which Jesus fed the four thousand was that it, like the other events, would have a vertical orientation to the direction of feeding. But for this event a vertical pattern (long side, or column, extending outward from Jesus with the feeding taking place from front to rear) refused to yield numerical values that fit in with the other events. Eventually, a horizontal pattern was considered for this case, which led to the inclusion of the parameter u in the analysis. With a horizontal pattern, the bread and fish were passed on in a direction at right angles to the orientation of the companies within the congregation, which remained constant throughout the feeding events. This pattern fit surprisingly well, and it fit only for the event of the four thousand. In regard to this parameter it is noted that there was one and only one valid orientation for each case, hinting that the exception itself favors the probability of design over chance in the differing orientations.

As the analysis proceeded, this difference in orientation was found to be of startling significance.

The second exception revealed that the individual patterns of Cases 2 and 3 did not result in the establishment of perfect rectangles as initially expected. However, the patterns of cases 1 and 2 combined to form the perfect complete rectangle initially assumed for each case, and the pattern of Case 3 produced two perfect rectangles, one of which was large and the other of which was much smaller. The combination of cases 1 and

2 represented an important suggestion that all the rectangles could be combined in some manner to yield a larger pattern, as described below.

The process described for Elisha's feeding event was remarkably similar to the accounts of Jesus' feeding of the multitudes. In fact, the numbers involved pointed to a configuration of 20 x 5 men, which furnished a prototype of the configuration of a company of 100 men, and justified the assumption made in the analysis that a company of 100 is arranged 20 x 5.

It did more than that. If Elisha's feeding of 100 is combined with Jesus' feeding of the 5000, it supplies the missing company of 100 for that account, creating in the combination a perfect rectangle of 5100 menfolk. This property, in turn, strongly suggested that all of the feeding incidents, including the feeding of the 4000, with its two perfect rectangles of 3850 and 150, may be combined in some meaningful way out of perfect rectangles.

These anomalies in the patterns, rather than indicating flaws in the Gospel accounts, suggest that their sequential linkage might combine into a composite pattern. This suggestion is given further credence in noting that the width of the pattern of Case 4 is identical to the width for Case 2.

When the operation of combining patterns, as suggested by these characteristics, was performed in the same sequence as the presentation of the events in the Bible, a composite pattern was indeed formed. That such a pattern existed was not an original objective, nor was it expected. It was found with astonishment that the exceptions described above were indispensible features of just such a composite pattern whose significance was immediately discernable. In retrospect, this integrating pattern seems to have been hinted at by Jesus in Mark 8.

The resulting pattern is a cross. The significance of the pattern was immediately apparent, revealing at once why the parameter u of the analysis not a constant over the events and why the rectangles had the precise shapes defined in the analysis.

The upper limb of this cross is furnished by Peter's three thousand; the lower limb is provided by Jesus' five thousand, and the crosspiece (patibulum) is represented by the horizontal bar of Jesus' four thousand. Although a variety of shapes have been suggested for the actual cross upon which Jesus was slain, the shape as depicted on the figure is the one which is most commonly associated with the event of His Passion.

The small rectangle formed from the extra three companies in Case 3 is interpreted as representing the sign, called the titulus, inscribed with the subject's name and supposed crime, which was attached to the cross along with the victim at the time of crucifixion. Jesus' titulus read "Jesus of Nazareth, King of the Jews" in three languages, as described in Luke

23:37. The languages written on it were Greek, Latin and Hebrew, all saying "This is the King of the Jews"

Interestingly the three languages on the titulus correspond to the three extra companies in case 3.

It is fascinating to note that if indeed Jesus' cross had been a Tau cross, as was commonly used by Romans at the time of Christ, then a simple rearrangement of the feeding patterns would furnish the associated representation. (See, for example, the article entitled "On the Physical Death of Jesus Christ" by William D. Edwards, MD, et al in the March 21, 1986 issue of JAMA.) For that period of time, the crosspiece (palibulum) was usually 5 to 6 feet in length, and the vertical post (stipes) was 6 to 8 feet in height. The average length ratio of palibulum to stipes for these ranges is (5/8+1)/2, or about 0.8 (.814). The length ratio of these members as derived from the analysis is nearly identical to this average, being approximately 0.8 (.8125).

PART SIX

THE ELUSIVE
REALITY OF UFOs

CHAPTER TWENTY

The Nature of the UFO

As a vague awareness of the possibility of UFO involvement in my life began to morph into a jarring sense of its likelihood, a growing curiosity over the UFO phenomenon led me to read of other tales. One recurring theme of the earlier modern phenomena that captured my interest was the involvement of Dr. J. Allen Hynek.

When Dr. Hynek agreed to work for the Air Force, he had no concept of the ride he had signed up for. Hired on in the '50s as a scientific consultant for Project Bluebook, the government-run clearing house for UFO incidents, he began delving into sighting reports with the materialistic no-nonsense mindset so common among scientists.

At first Dr. Hynek fit in perfectly with the project leaders and their prevailing skepticism, enthusiastically furnishing a number of highly creative quasi-scientific rational explanations for UFO sightings, all of which were meant to quell any notion that the phenomenon had a basis in the reality perceived by those who were making otherworld claims. Indeed, his 'swamp gas' explanation of some sightings became famous for arousing angry responses from UFO buffs and, for its basic unbelievability, implanting in their minds the first tangible indication of the possibility of a government cover-up.

Dr. Hynek didn't deserve their wrath. He was basically an honest and forthright man who understood the enormous potential impact of the UFO phenomenon on the prevailing naturalistic paradigm of the universe. He addressed his work with the utmost integrity; at the time he simply refused to believe in the supernatural, which to him was an essential feature of the sightings he had investigated. He had to furnish answers that made sense to him, and 'swamp gas' and the like were the best explanations he could come up with.

As he continued to pursue his investigations, however, his mind underwent a process of change. The witnesses were too credible to discount, their information too consistent, and their stories possessed a richness of new and unique information that smacked of truth. As Dr. Hynek began to appreciate the total inadequacy of his earlier explanations he listened with new ears to witness accounts. As time went on, he became much more sympathetic to them.

His intellect and scientific training led him to approach the UFO issue at a deeper level than many investigators. After he left Project Bluebook, he continued to pursue the UFO topic with great interest and wrote books on the subject. In his studies of UFO dynamics and behavior, he eventually reached a remarkable conclusion: in essence, the phenomena could not be understood or explained in terms of conventional physics: whatever was behind it must be spiritual in nature.

Of one thing Dr. Hynek was absolutely certain: whatever they might be, UFOs were real.

Regardless of what point of view, if any, we might choose to take regarding the existence of UFOs or their intent regarding the human race, a very large number of people already have been impacted by them, and the number grows larger every year. They avoid categorization; for every trait a sighting might possess, there seems to be an exception. Some may be perceived as good, but more are viewed as evil. Yet others are seen as pursuing a specific mission, and there are still other alien operations that are branded as irrational. Most are rather shy- sightings of them are rare enough that the majority of us are lucky to see one in a lifetime. But there are exceptions to that, too, a famous example being the Gulf Breeze Sightings that took place on the southwest region of Florida's panhandle near the Alabama border over a period of several years beginning November 11, 1987.

Ed Walters, a local building contractor, was a respected member of that residential community of about 6,000, which is situated on the western tip of a spit of land south of Pensacola. On that day in 1987 he happened to not only see the UFO but received esoteric information. He took Polaroid pictures of the device. The pictures were subsequently published in the Gulf Breeze Sentinel, which gave the event heavy local coverage. The sighting event included his getting zapped by a light beam from the craft that temporarily paralyzed him and lifted him off the ground, accompanied by a voice that said "don't worry, we won't harm you."

It would have been a fairly normal kind of UFO encounter if that had been all there was to it. But the sightings refused to stop. He had another one a week later. Then another. In fact, the number of sightings between November 1990 and July 1992 grew to over 150. The UFO occupants wouldn't let him alone, but continued to hound him until he became sick of the sightings and the attention he was getting and moved away.

That didn't end his involvement in the sightings. A model of a UFO was found in the attic of his old home. The "discovery" caused him to suddenly fall into disrepute, but subsequent findings led investigators away from seeing him in terms of culprithood. Instead, they began to sense his victimhood, perceiving him to be the subject of a well-planned attempt to discredit him, as discrepancies were found between the model and the photographs that he had taken of what he said were actual UFOs. In addition, he was investigated by Budd Hopkins and MUFON, respected UFO researchers who concluded that his sightings were not hoaxes. The investigation included two polygraph tests, the use of a tamper-proof camera, and investigation of corroborating witnesses, one of whom was an investigative psychologist and another of whom was an independent source of more pictures of the UFO.

Regardless of whether or not UFOs are accepted without doubt as real, the public attitude toward them is almost uniformly negative. But that is not always the case. What is certain is that the secular community perceives UFOs in a very different way than Christian communities should but do not. This is a sad situation, because some UFO sightings possess a religious element, particularly in the aftereffects. Moreover, it is in the religious context that the UFO phenomenon makes the most sense.

Accepting the reality of UFOs is comparable to believing in near-death experiences of heaven: people can indulge in endless speculation about them, but the truth of the matters can be fully understood only by those who have had actual experience with the events and their aftermaths. As for UFOs, their reality to me is a given, because I personally have experienced the event and the aftermath to me has been a glorious, life-changing journey. Apparently, the same can be said about many of those who have been on the edge between life and death and have returned back to this side.

CHAPTER TWENTY ONE

Opinions About UFOs

To some of our modern societies throughout the world, the reality of UFOs is a given; to others it is not. What is the attitude of those people who don't think UFOs exist? How about those who do? If the skeptics among us can be categorized as society's most rational, happy and well-adjusted, then we have good cause to wonder whether the entire phenomenon is self-generated and perhaps even delusional.

On the other hand, if the skeptics themselves are found to be lacking in those qualities, the case for the reality of UFOs is strengthened. Such was my mindset when I set out to connect the materialistic bias of the secular community with its attitude regarding UFOs.

There is a group within the secular community whose members are entirely indifferent to the UFO issue. This group can be categorized as consisting of imagination-challenged, intellectually shallow people who are focused on the mundane throughout their lives, being aware of only those events that might affect their own highly-developed self-interest. Not only is this camp indifferent to UFOs, it is also indifferent to the subject of God (except, perhaps as God might relate to Santa) and pretty much to anything not involving the next hamburger or the next episode of the Wheel. I dismiss it with a matching indifference.

The remainder of the secular world is divided into two sharply opposed camps regarding UFOs. A substantial segment of mainstream society, having bought into the prevailing secular paradigms of the world, places those who claim involvement in the UFO phenomenon as credulous, out of touch with reality, and rather on the fringe of social acceptability. Ironically, cutting-edge science is exposing the mainstream acceptance of basic secular paradigms, particularly of evolution, as credulous, naïve and all-too willing to embrace the myths fed them by agenda-based media. Nevertheless, these mainstreamers deny the existence of UFOs altogether, assuming that accounts of them originate with individuals who are burdened with problems of one sort or another. They are supported in large part by the mainstream media, the mainstream educational system, and mainstream science, to whom they prefer for answers to their own minds and common sense. This group, being marginally more intelligent, are marginally more aware of the world about them than those who are completely indifferent to the UFO phenomenon. They also are marginally more interesting.

The opposing secular camp not only believes in the existence of UFOs, but sees in them an alien presence, irrelevant to God, that has invaded us both now and in the past. This more interesting group consists of those who not only believe in UFOs, but acknowledge their historical existence and generally think that they are up to no good. Investigators within the camp of historical or ancient encounters are represented by authors Erich Von Daniken, Zecharia Sitchin and Robert Temple. The more speculative details presented by them include mythological connections to Sirius or alien visitors in our past who came from an unknown planet of a highly eccentric orbit within our own solar system, their orbit keeping them from observation except at very rare intervals. There are a number of investigative organizations such as MUFON that focus on more modern sightings. Information on them can be readily acquired on the Internet. We shall set aside the speculative details as interesting but somewhat irrelevant to a demonstration of the reality of extraterrestrial visitors. For the most part we will confine our attention here to the core issue of the reality of past and present visitations to earth by extraterrestrial beings, whatever their possible origins. The basic questions alone raise a variety of issues important to the speculative Christian.

If there is reality behind the UFO phenomenon – and that's a very big if to the secular mind – the perception of their craft is consistently viewed in naturalistic terms. Whether they come from a different planet or galaxy, UFOs belong to the same universe as we inhabit, along with our own dimensional constraints. The craft, to them, are electromechanical devices like our own aircraft and space vehicles but designed and fabricated with the aid of a technology that is more advanced than ours. The implications of this standard perception have both technical and social components.

Technically, we are intrigued with the capabilities of UFOs, because evidence of their existence includes features such as their maneuverability, speed, power source, mode of overcoming gravity, and electromagnetic effects when they are in proximity to our own vehicles and appliances that extend rather far beyond our own capabilities in these areas. Some individuals would welcome contact with UFO occupants for the superior knowledge that they might be able to impart to us and thereby raise us up to new levels more compatible with their own. Such individuals are in the minority due to the social implications noted below.

The social implications of a more advanced society go beyond perceptions of UFO occupants as alien beings. Whether they are similar to us or not, their presence on earth represents *de facto* superiority. We know from experience within our own human society that when two peoples of unequal civilizations meet, they will clash, with the more advanced civilization dominating and eventually destroying the less developed one. This understanding is not lost on those who contemplate a future world in which UFO occupants would openly interact with humanity, and the thought is sufficient to generate real fear. This perceived threat to our way of life and even to our own continued existence would be more than sufficient to erect a governmental barrier of secrecy around the UFO phenomenon and to downplay the existence of such to the general public.

It is becoming evident from this very brief discussion that responses of interest, particularly within the prevailing secular element of society, tend toward negative viewpoints. One might readily infer from this that the mainstream media, dominated by the secular outlook, may not be overly forthcoming to the public, and its agenda is supported by a good percentage of society which has neither the mental nor emotional wherewithal to withstand their lack of candor regarding UFOs (and a number of other topics as well). It is the skeptics themselves and the public institutions that formulate reality in their behalf who lack credibility.

Difficulties have surfaced for a materialistic view of UFOs. At the outset of the modern sightings the confusing and improbable features of UFOs raised a number of questions relating to the technology that aliens might possess to enable them to perform the radical maneuvers associated with them or their vehicles. Over the several decades that have passed since the first well-publicized modern sightings in 1947, it was recognized that technology alone furnished an insufficient explanation of their characteristics and capabilities, which led a number of researchers in that field to question whether the aliens might have a spiritual quality. The mindset of Dr. J. Allen Hyneck, who came into the field of UFO investigations as a consultant to the U.S. Air Force's Project Bluebook, changed over the course of his investigations from skeptic to believer in the alien hypothesis, but he went beyond the extraterrestrial notion to a belief in something perhaps more spiritual in the nature of the alien beings than the common understanding admits. Jacques Vallee, a long-time UFO investigator who has gained a considerable measure of respect in the field, echoes this thought.

In his 1988 book *Dimensions,* Vallee asserts that UFO visitations, with many of their modern characteristics, have been with us since the beginning of mankind's civilization. He traces the evidence for this assertion throughout our history, noting the many famous sightings which extend past a number of recorded incidents from the present down through the middle ages into antiquity. Most important to our subject, he cites the numerous Biblical passages such as the vision of Ezekiel, which overtly refer to such visitations as having a distinct religious flavor wherein the UFO aspect merges into Judeo-Christian canon. Moreover, he notes, the nature of these visitations, in which the 'beings' appear to be beyond the constraints of mass, space, and time in their ability to levitate, withstand radical maneuvers, and pass through solid objects, possess the same features that make the modern UFO sightings so enigmatic. It is these disturbing characteristics which so oppose modern rationalist thinking, Vallee claims, that put the UFO 'occupants' into a category beyond the mere extraterrestrial. He speculates on the possibility that they might be interdimensional, occupying a universe parallel to our own.

In general, troubled and partially-formulated speculations like Vallee's serve to emphasize the ultra-rigid boundaries of the modern rationalist way of thinking. The notion of a spirit-based entity capable of passing through solid objects is usually rejected quite rapidly as ridiculous. The assertion of this as impossible in our 'real' world also denies the possibility that the soul, so important to the Christian belief, can exist. A passage in Chapter 20 of John's Gospel as noted previously directly refutes this denial. In that passage the resurrected Jesus performs the same acts that the UFO debunker uses to discredit the reality of UFO sightings.

In the passage referred to above, Jesus not only passed through solid walls to appear to the disciples, but presented the form of flesh to Thomas. He also ate with them. These capabilities that include the materialistic but extend beyond materialism are precisely those characteristics of many UFO sightings that cause such consternation among the investigators and their audience. Yet many of our cutting-edge physicists confront these mysterious capabilities on a daily basis in their investigations into quantum physics.

CHAPTER TWENTY TWO

Typical UFO Encounters

This chapter will look at several modern UFO incidents as typical encounters whose events and the affected subjects give us enough rational information to support the claim that UFOs do indeed exist. These particular incidents are dated, but don't differ much from more up-to-date sightings. They have the advantage of novelty, so the accounts carry with them little of the baggage of bias associated with UFOs.

The search for rationality in them is a daunting objective, as many modern UFO sightings share few traits that don't vary over time and events. Despite common core features that tempt investigators to treat as "classic" characteristics, the objects will then deviate from the pattern in follow-on sightings; they adhere to a pattern which appears for a time to be typical, but will then change. The most basic characteristic of the UFO is that it doesn't play fair – it doesn't follow our rules for rational behavior. Perhaps this is its most invariant characteristic – its propensity to vary. This irritating feature has driven a number of modern scientists away from the ranks of the believers, as the scientific holy grail of repeatability appears to be violated at every turn.

UFOs refuse to stand still to be inspected, classified, and catalogued. When we label them as disc-shaped, they show up in the new cigar model. When we note that they are only passively observing, people start claiming abduction. We jokingly create a scenario where they say 'take me to your leader', and they engage in a mass overflight of Washington, D. C. We study and measure the imprints of their landing gear, and we start getting crop circles in return. Those individuals who have undertaken to study their behavior from a secular, mechanistic perspective have not yet been able to definitively discern the logic behind it. How can they? Whatever logic might be behind the sightings appears to be as alien to us as the occupants and their craft.

It's all very frustrating. No self-respecting scientist appreciates being toyed with by the object of his investigation. It is so much better for the ego to simply claim that the UFOs, along with their aberrant behavior, are products of deranged imaginations. It is better yet to lump the numerous religious elements in with the UFO "fantasy" itself.

Unfortunately for such skeptics, that isn't the whole story by any means. In the context of Christianity, many of the cases that might seem bizarre to the secularist fit well into the Scriptural narrative. There is another group of people as well who appreciate the reality and seriousness of UFOs. Removed from the popular façade of skepticism and indifference, scientists within this other group devote their lives to the study of UFOs. They just aren't in the public sector; they work for governments, and their work is secret. Governments are quite concerned over the matter, because these 'things', whatever they are, cannot be controlled by them.

The following sighting reports extracted from a number of sources typify the behavior of the craft and occupants over a period now extending over several decades. Although many of these seem to be rather old by secular standards, they also typify more recent sightings. Moreover, given the relative newness of the topic in these reports, attitudes toward the objects don't reflect the entrenched opinions associated with later reports. The reports support their reality, particularly with respect to electromagnetic effects and in the degree of governmental concern, but they also demonstrate how very elusive the UFOs are, and how helpless we are to do anything about them.

Report #1 – The UFO Casebook, Captain Kevin D. Randle, USAF, Ret., Warner Books, 1989

This incident involves a highly-controversial UFO event that continues to be hotly debated to this day, over a quarter of a century later. It is certainly among the ten most famous cases of all time, and is arguably the most important. Much of the controversy surrounding it is due to strong evidence of a governmental cover-up of the issue.

The event itself is described beginning on page 5 under the heading "July 2, 1947: Roswell, New Mexico;" the cover-up aftermath begins on page 16 under the heading "September 24, 1947: The Majestic Twelve". Referring to his first account of the event, Randle claimed that rumors of wreckage from crashed UFOs followed Kenneth Arnold's first sighting.

According to Randle, these stories were not taken seriously, belonging more to the genre of science fiction than reality. Given the prevailing lack of proof, researchers took them to be nothing more than hoaxes until the first rumors were came out in 1980 regarding a crash in the vicinity of Roswell, New Mexico. Even then, reaction to the Roswell crash initially continued to be met with skepticism.

Yet the situation at Roswell was different than its predecessors, Randle claimed. He noted that this time witnesses were available who described a disc-shaped object suffering stability problems that eventually exploded upon crashing, and government documents hinted that something real involving a UFO had taken place here. According to a local newspaper article, rancher William (Mac) Brazel found odd debris on his property and evidence that the wreckage was incomplete. When he examined the pieces they appeared to possess properties suggesting a technology that went beyond that possessed by present-day humanity.

Brazel notified the newspaper and sheriff in Roswell. Word spread to the nearby Roswell Army Air Field, causing Major Jesse Marcel to investigate the scene of the crash. Marcel contacted Colonel William Blanchard after collecting samples of the debris. Blanchard, in turn, told Lieutenant William Haut to release a statement confirming the recovery of wreckage from a disc that had crashed in the local area. The wreckage retrieved by Marcel was taken to the distant Carswell Air Force Base in Fort Worth. It's ultimate destination was Wright Field in Ohio, where the transfer took place under the watchful eyes of guards. At another news conference, the official story claimed a misidentification of the UFO with that of a weather balloon. Meanwhile, the Army held Brazel for almost a week during a thorough examination of the crash site. He was released on the condition of his complete silence on the matter.

Another crash site was reported closely on the heel of this incident, this time near Magdalena, New Mexico. Witness Grady L. Barnett also claimed to have found the crashed remains of a disc-shaped craft.

"While he was examining it," Randall notes, "a small group of people arrived who said they were part of an archeological research team from the University of Pennsylvania.

"Barnett recalled that they were all standing around looking at bodies that had fallen to the ground. He thought there were others in the machine, and that all the creatures were dead. He tried to get closer. He described them as humanoid with round heads, small eyes, and no hair. All were dressed in gray, one-piece suits that didn't have zippers or buttons or belts. Barnett claimed that he was close enough to touch them, but didn't. The military had arrived, taken charge, and escorted him away."

Once again, Air Force investigators arrived at the crash site and claimed the debris, committing Barnett, like Brazel, to silence under the threat of severe penalties.

Captain Randle continues with the account, the highlights including Marcel's adamant conviction that the object he saw and the associated wreckage that he handled wasn't that of a weather balloon. In fact, Marcel was so angry with the explanation that he "stormed into Blanchard's office demanding a court martial". He was sent on leave the next day.

Our overview of the Roswell incident turns next to the follow-on account involving a bizarre, secretive group labeled "The Majestic Twelve", as narrated again by Captain Randle under the subtitle "September 24, 1947: The Majestic Twelve":

"Shortly after the Roswell disc was recovered, and the wreckage moved to Wright Field, President Truman realized that he would need a panel of experts to study the wreckage and the phenomena. Code-named Majestic Twelve or MJ-12, the group as formed on September 24, 1947, by then President Truman. When Eisenhower was elected in 1952, a top-secret document was prepared for him. Portions of that document received by researchers mention the Roswell crashed disc and state that four alien bodies were recovered."

Randle adds that in a report that surfaced in 1980 mention was made of the MJ-12, confirming the existence of that group.

In addition, he notes that General Hoyt S. Vandenburg, who was listed as a member of MJ-12, downplayed the existence of the UFO and ordered the destruction of all copies of the report. According to Randle another member of MJ-12 was Lloyd Berkner, who also was a member of the Robertson Panel that attempted to discredit the reality of the UFO phenomenon.

Randle continued to suggest that the U. S. government actively attempted to tamp down the credibility of UFO sightings. "During the 1950s," he states, "as the various evidences of UFO sightings were ridiculed, one of the most famous of the debunkers was Donald Menzel. He wrote books pointing out how rational, intelligent observers could be fooled by the usual seen under unusual circumstances. He reported in one of his books that the Tremonton film had been proven, conclusively, to be birds seen at the very limit of the visual range.

"J. Allen Hynek, while watching the film twenty years later, was heard to exclaim incredulously, 'Birds! Birds?' Hynek didn't expect that answer. In fact, anyone who had seen the film would wonder how a scientist of Menzel's stature could accept an explanation that is so obviously a label slapped on to identify the film rather than let it linger in the public mind.

"Menzel is listed as a member of the Majestic Twelve."

Captain Randle then lists the original members of the MJ-2 panel and comments that every time an investigation of a UFO incident is sidetracked, hampered or debunked there seemed to be a link to MJ-12. He concedes, however, that there appear to be some unresolved inconsistencies in attempts to prove the existence of the group. As for the incident itself, its features include the following:

> Actual physical evidence of a UFO, including strange materials and bodies.

> The occurrence of a crash, indicating the imperfection of the craft and supporting the notion that the UFO possessed features that were compatible with our material domain.

> The existence of dead alien bodies, indicating that the occupants of the craft also either belonged in or could enter our physical universe.

> Evidence that the government has been engaging in cover-up of UFO incidents.

> Rational explanations other than a UFO do exist, and could explain the governmental secrecy as well. Foremost among these is the possibility that the craft was a highly-secret advanced experimental aircraft. However, it is doubtful that the kind of technology associated with the Roswell craft existed in 1947. And what about the bodies?

> That there has been a governmental cover-up is less doubtful. Please refer below to Chapter Twenty Three: Fraudulent debunking – methodology and famous episodes.

Report #2 – The UFO Conspiracy, Jenny Randles, Barnes & Noble, 1987

In Chapter 5 of her book *The UFO Conspiracy*, Jenny Randles begins her description of a 1952 incident with a tongue-in-cheek flavor:

"In those early years of the UFO phenomenon, one cry was often heard. If UFOs are real, why don't they show themselves to everyone and land on the White House lawn? Indeed, that theme was woven into several science-fiction movies in the first half of the 1950s. In the summer of 1952, science-fiction almost became a reality.

"With Project Grudge on hold, the Air Force was officially no longer interested in the subject. Yet behind the scenes there was frantic activity. Intelligence Officer Captain Edward J. Ruppelt had been assigned to reshape the study and field the mounting concern within the Pentagon. That was October 1951. By March 1952 his recommendations for a new project were accepted and the code name Project Blue Book was assigned to it. Ruppelt, who quickly became convinced of UFO reality and often investigated cases on his own initiative and even at his own expense, says the title was based on a college exam paper filled with tough questions."

At the outset of Project Blue Book the number of sightings was small, with an uptick in May 1952 producing 79. According to Randles, this was just the start of a massive wave, with 149 cases in June and 700 over the July-August period. Some of the witnesses to these sightings in which Ruppelt was involved were fighter pilots who had fired on the UFOs. Their reports were never publicized. Becoming increasingly frustrated over the apparent government unwillingness to make public the results of whatever investigations they actually pursued, Ruppelt eventually left the Air Force.

Randles then described the shocking event that can best be characterized as an actual "Take us to your leader" situation. She noted that on July 19, 1952 radar at a commercial airport at Washington, D. C. (unspecified but probably Reagan-Washington National) picked up a formation of seven objects close to Andrews Air Force Base. The controller on duty initially considered them to be military traffic as they moved at a speed consistent with known aircraft. As there was not supposed to be such traffic there he was alerted to a potential problem. His puzzlement turned to astonished concern as two of the objects accelerated to a speed outside the limit of capability of known aircraft. He was accompanied by his senior controller and two other experienced radar operators, all of whom confirmed the remaining blips but were unable to offer a solution to the enigma. Their radar sighting was confirmed by a second radar located in a different building, whose operators corroborated the same incident. The event was corroborated further by radar operators at Andrews Air Force Base.

Randles continued with the comment that "For three radar systems all to be recording this dramatic 'invasion' of the nation's capital was immediately significant. They knew a systems malfunction could not be to blame, but Barnes ordered his radar checked anyway. There were no faults. Meanwhile the targets had moved at speeds up to 7000 mph, before stopping rapidly and then cruising about, behaviour patterns never witnessed before by any of the experts. What is more, they had intruded upon restricted air space – taking them right over the White House."

Commenting on the efforts of the Air Force to keep this situation out of the press, Randles notes the shabby treatment given Ruppelt, the investigator at the time. "Ruppelt . . . was not even granted a staff car to interview the scattered witnesses. Use the bus, he was told! Then he was advised that he was spending too much time away from Wright Patterson (the UFO project home base) and if he did not get back he would be reported AWOL!"

Randles continued with this tale, because it was not yet over. Another UFO overflight of Washington, D.C. occurred a week later, accompanied by bureaucratic indifference or worse, in which Ruppelt was deliberately cut out of the informational loop.

Significant feature of the sightings include the following elements:

Combined radar/visual sightings were involved

There were multiple related incidents

The objects exhibited what have come to be labeled as classic UFO maneuvers that exceed our own current capabilities; these maneuvers included sudden acceleration and deceleration, changes in direction, hovering, and vanishing.

There is evidence that the government deliberately downplayed and even attempted to cover up the incidents.

Report #3 – UFO Briefing Document, Don Berliner, Dell 1995

This report is a sighting involving multiple witnesses in November, 1957 around Levelland, Texas. According to Don Berliner, the Project Blue Book report attributed the [multiple-witness] sighting to an over-reaction to a severe electrical storm.

"At 10:30 p.m. came the report from truck driver Pedro Saucedo, who described seeing a blue torpedo-shaped object with yellow flame and white smoke coming out of its rear. He estimated it was 200 feet long and 6 feet wide. He said it rose from a nearby field and roared low over his truck with a loud, explosive sound, and produced so much heat he got out of his truck and [laid] on the ground. 'It sounded like thunder, and my truck rocked from the blast.' He thought it came within 200-300 feet. His truck lights and engine failed while the UFO was in view; after it disappeared, his lights worked perfectly, and he was able to re-start the engine."

As Berliner notes, the event didn't stop there. As the UFO flew past a farm ten miles to the northwest, the engines of two grain combines went dead. Then around midnight a large, elliptical-shaped UFO landed on a road, causing the headlights and engine of Jim Wheeler's car to stop working as he approached it. They resumed working when the UFO rose and flew off. The same thing happened to Jose Alvarez's car.

That still wasn't the end of the event. Also around midnight, Newell Wright's car stopped working as well. Berliner relates what happened. "He got out to fix them, looked up and saw a glowing, bluish-green, flat-bottomed, oval object on the highway. The object was in sight for four or five minutes. During that time, Wight tried to start his engine, and while the starter made contact, the motor was unaffected. The object disappeared, straight up, and immediately the car lights came back on, the engine started, and then operated perfectly."

About a half hour later, Frank Williams experienced the same problem with a glowing, egg-shaped UFO. Then just after that, Ronald Martin's truck stopped in the presence of a round, glowing UFO, which changed in color from orange to blue-green upon landing. After it took off, the engine started by itself. After two more people had associated UFO flyovers with operational difficulties with their vehicles, county Sheriff Weir Clem drove out to see for himself what was happening. He saw a huge, football-shaped UFO traveling at an incredible rate. His car continued to run.

Common features include:

> There were multiple related incidents and associated multiple witnesses

> Automotive electrical systems failed in every incident except one when the UFO approached

> The objects exhibited what have come to be labeled as classic UFO maneuvers that exceed our own current capabilities; these maneuvers included sudden acceleration and deceleration, changes in direction, hovering, and vanishing.

Report #4 – UFO Casebook, Kevin Randle, Warner 1989

An account similar to the previous report is given by Kevin Randle in *The UFO Casebook*. He adds that the Levelland events were just a part of a larger wave of sightings which extended over a broad area and included close encounters and other physical effects.

At the Project Bluebook office in Dayton, Ohio, the incident began with a chattering teletype. The sheriff in the previous report had called in the sightings to Reese Air Force Base in Lubbock, Texas, who then notified the Bluebook personnel. At Bluebook, they quickly came to the conclusion that the sightings were caused by ball lightning associated with sever thunderstorms in the area. They pinned the failed engines on over-excited drivers, who somehow in the heat of the moment, turned off their ignition switches. If that was what actually happened, the investigators who made this claim never bothered to question what had gotten the multiple drivers so agitated as to do such a thing. According to Randle, the event was further complicated by an additional report from two men on patrol at White Sands who witnessed an egg-shaped UFO. This was followed by a second report from a different patrol in that area with a similar account.

At about the same time as the Levelland sightings, James Stokes, who was employed at the Holloman Air Force Base, experienced the usual car trouble near Orogrande, New Mexico. After his car stopped running, he observed a number of people pointing to the sky. When he followed their outstretched hands, he also saw a large oval UFO, which made two passes over the highway before vanishing. Stokes felt heat as the object passed overhead, and hours later experienced itching on his exposed flesh. When he reported the incident to the Air Force, they subjected him to a harsh interview, probably intended to corroborate a news release to the effect that the alleged sightings were misinterpreted natural phenomena. Nevertheless, the Air Force reported Stokes to be a credible witness. During that time, yet another person came forward, reporting to the police at Kearney, Nebraska that he had been paralyzed by a beam of light from a UFO. After searching him for weapons, the occupants of the craft invited R. O. Schmidt to come aboard. Two women and three men inside were working on what he supposed was instrumentation.

A number of similar reports followed on the heels of Schmidt's experience, involving occupants of the craft, who talked with at least one witness.

Randle continues to describe a number of additional sightings around the country in that same time period, several of which involved encounters with the occupants of the craft.

There are several interesting features associated with the Levelland and associated events:

> The objects had a variety of oval, spherical, and triangular shapes.

> They were sighted by multiple witnesses over different locations and times. Some of the sightings included occupants; others

generated heat felt by the witnesses, followed by burns and rashes.

Most, but not all, witnesses described what may be considered a temporary electromagnetic impact on their vehicles.

The associated light and maneuvers inspired awe.

Finally, and as an important corroboration of the necessity for independent thought, the governmental authority (U. S. Air Force) attempted to publicly discredit the sightings.

Report #5 – UFO Briefing Document, Don Berliner, Dell 1995

This case is summarized in a memo from Commander-in-Charge, NORAD, dated 11 Nov. 1975. The memo listed a large number of Air Force bases since the previous month reporting UFOs to NORAD, including Loring in Maine, Wurtsmith in Michigan, Malmstrom in Montana, Minot in North Dakota, and a Canadian base in Falconbridge, Ontario. The report from Malmstrom had characterized the sound of the object as similar to a jet, although there were no known jets in the area. The object was confirmed by Malmstrom radar. Fighter jets were scrambled but could not make contact. On November 10, a bright car-sized UFO noiselessly buzzed the base. The next morning Falconbridge in Canada reported a radar and visual sighting of an object about a hundred feet in diameter pocked with craters on its surface.

The NORAD memo expressed concern about the inability so far to positively identify the craft.

A number of interesting facts may be gleaned from this report:

This report was written in 1975, six years after the controversial Condon Report was completed, finding in contradiction to its own data that UFOs were perceived to be no threat to national security. The Air Force discontinued all public UFO data-gathering projects after the issuance of the Condon Report.

This report expressed concern over a number of sightings in the vicinity of nuclear missile installations.

The report was written by a senior Air Force official, responsible for the air defense of the United States. His reliability was sound, and his consternation was not trivial.

The objects were sighted visually and on radar. Fighter jets were scrambled to intercept them.

The objects were characterized by bright light, odd maneuver patterns, and intermittency of contact. This intermittency suggests that the objects were capable of entering and leaving our normal space/time dimensions.

The commander who wrote the report was concerned about preventing a public reaction to the sightings. This is highly significant in corroborating the suspicion of government motives regarding the defunct Air Force sighting projects.

Report #6 – UFO Briefing Document, Don Berliner, Dell 1995

Another military sighting occurred at a Soviet base on July 28, 1989. The report is from one of multiple witnesses, as was extracted from KGB files. A companion report of the same incident noted that a fighter was scrambled to intercept it. As related to Berliner, the craft emitted a brilliant flashing light as it flew over the logistics yard, heading toward the nearby rocket weapons depot. When it reached the depot, it hovered over it. The UFO had a diameter of about fifteen feet and was of the usual half-spherical saucer shape. The hull was dimly lighted with a green hue.

The UFO emitted a bright beam from the bottom as it hovered over the depot. It then moved back over the logistics yard, then the railway, and a cement factory before returning to the rocket weapons depot, where it remained for about two hours. After that it flew off in the direction of Akhtubinsk.

This report tells us that:

It was a multiple-witness sighting.

The sighting occurred at a military base, in which missiles were stored.

The UFO was disc-shaped and exhibited a classic maneuver pattern.

The Soviet government had sufficient interest in the sighting to scramble an interceptor after it, and to document the case.

Report #7 – Dimensions, Jacques Vallee, Ballantine

There are many cases in the UFO literature of encounters that go beyond mere sightings to actual abductions. In his book *Dimensions*, Jacques Vallee summarizes the case of Barney and Betty Hill, whose encounter arguably places it into the ten most famous abduction events of all time.

The couple were returning in their car from a vacation in September 1961 when they saw what seemed to them to be an odd light coming close to them as they traveled over a deserted stretch of road over the White Mountains. Their next awareness was inside their car sixty miles to the south. After their return home, they experienced thoughts that were troubling enough to lead them to a psychiatrist who examined them under hypnosis. The hypnosis evoked lengthy tales of a UFO abduction that included the examination of their bodies by small beings whose expressions were similar to those of humans. The occupants communicated by means of an unknown language. They could discern no pattern or rational purpose behind the experience.

The 'medical examinations' appear to be a common feature of abductions. Another common feature of abductions is that the experience leaves a lasting impression on the witness, affecting him long after the occurrence of the sighting event.

With respect to the persistence of long-range effects, this report is similar to my own experience, as related in Parts One through Five above; however, my personal experience differed from this report in that mine did indeed have a meaningful purpose, was positive, and had religious connotations.

Other commonalities include the following.

It was a multiple-witness sighting.

The UFO was disc-shaped, larger than any known man-made flying vehicle, and performed maneuvers that may be considered common to UFOs.

The UFO occupants had the ability to communicate telepathically with the witness.

Report #8 – Dimensions, Jacques Vallee, Ballantine

As dairy farmer Gary Wilcox approached a field to check on ground conditions, he observed what he thought to be a refrigerator or some other object discarded on his field. As he got closer to it, he saw it to be an egg-shaped metallic device of sixteen by twenty foot size. It was cool to the touch. Despite the apparent absence of doors, two small creatures looking like humans appeared as if out of nowhere. They communicated with him but not with their mouths. After reassuring him that they had no hostile intent, they told him they were from Mars, and that environmental conditions there were forcing them to adopt new agricultural techniques that they hoped to borrow from those on Earth. They were particularly interested in Gary's fertilizers. Their conversation with him left him with the impression that they didn't know much about farming. He walked away to get a bag of fertilizer when they asked him for it, but they were gone when he returned. He left the bag in the field, and it was no longer there the next morning. They also told Wilcox that the human body would never adapt to space.

Go figure. It would be very interesting to know if this witness underwent a long-term mental or intellectual impact of a more serious and comprehensible nature quite apart from the absurdity of the initial encounter. Mr. Vallee cites many other incomprehensible encounters, both ancient and modern. In *Dimensions*, he establishes past UFO experience as the substance of legends, even with magic and religion. He links UFOs with the fairies, elves, dwarfs, gnomes, 'little people', and 'good people' of folklore.

What hasn't been covered in this very abbreviated presentation of some interesting sightings is the several accounts of crashed UFOs, including their occupants, which extend all the way back to the time frame of Kenneth Arnold's experience. Such incidents are simply beyond the scope of this essay. Our plate is full enough revisiting some of the more mundane sightings without attempting to assess the reality of this more exotic type of event. If there is truth to these stories, however, would the existence of such physical evidence place the UFO firmly in the extraterrestrial category and out of the domain of the spiritual? I would say no; that does not necessarily follow. Those among us who are not inclined toward religion tend to place the domain of God in the spiritual realm, away from our everyday reality. If there are some religious connotations to the UFO matter, and there seems to be evidence of that, I would remind the reader that the Judeo-Christian God, at least, has identified Himself as the Creator of the physical universe and all that is within it. In that context, the existence of direct physical evidence of the UFO is actually quite compatible with the possibility of a religious dimension.

A summary of these sighting reports follows:

The objects maneuver in patterns that don't conform to our large-body physics. They appear to have the ability to enter and leave our space/time continuum.

The occupants appear to be interested in our technology and advancements, especially in the military field.

Sightings are world-wide in scope. They haven't stopped, despite the alleged government lack of interest. The U.S. government, in fact, appears to be deliberately misleading its public regarding this issue.

Sightings can be intensely personal to the viewers, even to the point of altering lives. This alteration can be both negative and positive. In some cases, the primary impact occurs after a considerable time has elapsed since the overt sighting. Some experiences have religious connotations.

The UFOs appear to possess physical attributes to the extent that they appear to be metallic and solid, are seen visually and have an electromagnetic influence on equipment, including vehicles and radar.

There appears to be governmental involvement in the UFO phenomenon. The government appears to be withholding information from the public of the matter while conducting an intense, behind-the-scenes investigation on its own. As noted in Chapter Twenty Three, it appears to be rather obvious that there is indeed a fraudulent debunking effort in which the government is participating. It appears to have been successful, at least as far as the mainstream press and networks are concerned: while sightings continue unabated as can be gleaned from Internet accounts, they very rarely reach the public via the traditional media.

CHAPTER TWENTY THREE

Fraudulent UFO Reporting

Many attempts to debunk the UFO issue have been exposed as fraudulent. This chapter examines the methodology of the fraud and relates famously sordid episodes, which serve, in direct opposition to their original intent, to corroborate the basic reality of the UFO phenomenon.

In reviewing the UFO controversy to date, one cannot help but have the impression that while the public has been given one version of the story, officialdom has kept to itself quite another. That the popular media followed an intentional plan to discredit the subject is possibly open to question. Nevertheless, the fact is that with the help of 'official' attempts to discredit the UFO phenomenon, they have performed a magnificent job of overly sensationalizing and otherwise trivializing the UFO situation. Serious researchers, on the other hand, acknowledge that the weight of evidence very definitely points to the reality of the objects, the intelligence behind their design, and their non-human origin. What is more disconcerting is that this view is apparently shared behind the scenes by government officials, some of whom have encouraged an overt debunking of the entire matter. Some high officials, even U.S. Presidents, have been bold enough to speak publicly of their beliefs in the reality of UFOs. Apparently, however, they have been unable to influence the secret policies of the unelected bureaucracies. Consider, for example, what Victor Marchetti, a former official in the CIA, had to say about government policy regarding the treatment of UFO data and the increasing cynicism it engendered in the public mind in a 1985 address:

"We have, indeed been contacted – perhaps even visited – by extraterrestrial beings, and the U.S. government, in collusion with the other national powers of the earth, is determined to keep this information from the general public.

"The purpose of the international conspiracy is to maintain a workable stability among the nations of the world and for them, in turn, to retain institutional control over their respective populations. Thus, for these governments to admit that there are beings from outer space . . . with mentalities and technological capabilities obviously far superior to ours, could, once fully perceived by the average person, erode the foundations of the earth's traditional power structure. Political and legal systems, religions, economic and social institutions could all soon become meaningless in the mind of the public. The national oligarchic establishments, even civilization as we now know it, could collapse into anarchy.

"Such extreme conclusions are not necessarily valid, but they probably accurately reflect the fears of the 'ruling classes' of the major nations, whose leaders (particularly those in the intelligence business) have always advocated excessive governmental secrecy as being necessary to preserve the 'national security'."

Actually, Marchetti's conjecture is not universally valid. Other governments, particularly France and Belgium, have been more open to their public with regard to the reporting of sighting information and disseminating the results of investigations. Apparently, the United States government is among the more repressive national authorities in this regard.

The *UFO Briefing Document* compiled by Don Berliner, who also noted Marchetti's address, cites four Presidents, four congresspersons, six generals, one admiral, and six astronauts from the United States alone who have considered the UFO topic serious enough to speak out publicly about it. Individuals of this caliber did not reach their positions of public trust through an inability to think for themselves. In fact, the situation may be exactly the reverse. Could the American public have been so intellectually shallow as to have unquestioningly swallowed the trivialization and 'official' debunking of the subject? According to polls in which anonymity is maintained, the public has not swallowed the official line. Given the apparent difference between its private beliefs and those which it is willing to share with others, the public simply lacks the moral courage to openly express itself in matters that are perceived to oppose the current fashion.

It was sufficient, in the creation of a taboo against the belief in UFOs, for the 'official' policy to establish the fashion.

The several U.S. Air Force projects, beginning with Project Sign in 1948, which ostensibly attempted to document and investigate UFO sightings in America, exhibit such a poorly-disguised attempt at disinformation that anyone capable of thinking for himself should be skeptical of the Air Force intent with respect to informing the public. In several cases, the information given to the public through these 'official' projects has been openly self-contradictory. Concern over this misleading information has been voiced over the years by a number of high ranking officials throughout the world. There is evidence that the best UFO sighting data was not included in the project databases. In fact, it was rather plainly stated in Air Force reporting directives that 'hard' information was to be passed on to other government channels for processing.

A commentary by Jacques Vallee in *Dimensions* regarding the handling of a 1965 sighting typifies the attitude taken by investigators for Project Blue Book and the reliability of the media. When Dr. Hynek had heard from Vallee of the Michigan sightings at that time, he called Project Blue Book, pushing them to investigate before any evidence was destroyed by reporters and the curious. According to Hynek, the Blue Book case officer was indifferent, telling Hynek that the events hadn't been officially reported to the Air Force. When Hynek responded with the comment that he wasn't being very scientific, the case officer shot back with an expletive to the effect that he didn't care. But then he called back about a half hour later requesting Hynek to investigate the incident himself. It turned out that the Pentagon called the Air Force about the UFO situation after being inundated with calls from reporters across the country. Hynek went to Ann Arbor where he spoke to the press, who wanted immediate answers. As he spoke about the need for a thorough investigation, he let slip a comment that some of the sightings may have been caused by swamp gas. The press blew that statement all out of proportion in an indignant and very hypocritical anger at Hynek's very premature statement. It was the press itself that had ridiculed UFO sighting events in the past.

In *The UFO Casebook*, former U.S. Air Force officer Kevin Randle attempts to tie up the loose ends of many well-known past UFO sightings. His additional research has exposed several hoaxes. But Captain Randle has also exposed evidence, some subtle and other quite overt, of intentional governmental cover-up. One often-used trick, he noted, is to embellish straightforward accounts of sightings with enough false information of an absurd nature to thoroughly discredit them.

It is one thing for an individual to report that he had seen an egg-shaped craft darting about in the sky, performing seemingly impossible maneuvers. It is quite another to add that the craft landed and out popped three Venusians with purple wings, claiming via telepathic communication that they are emissaries to our planet seeking to help us obtain membership in the galactic civilization. If indeed the government is pursuing this kind of policy, the current timidity with which the man on the street regards the UFO experience indicates that this ploy has been quite successful in marginalizing the entire affair.

There are other tricks in the debunking bag that the government has apparently used quite often in the past: delaying an investigation until the memory of an event has blurred in the witness' minds, the physical evidence has been compromised, and key witnesses are no longer available; ignoring an event altogether; planting false evidence at a site; confiscating evidence; intimidating witnesses; and improperly linking the sighting with natural events that may have occurred at the same time. As to whether these tactics were employed intentionally or merely out of incompetence, Randle points out that in 1953 the Robertson Panel secretly recommended such a policy. According to him, the panel itself hinted at the use of debunking to reduce the public interest in UFOs and thereby lessen the danger of widespread psychological reactions. Labeling this process "education", they noted that it could be accomplished through television, film and articles in magazines and newspapers. Such "information", according to them, would be useful in reducing the public's gullibility and susceptibility to hostile propaganda.

Ironically, the 'gullible public' may just be that segment which is so incapable of thinking for itself that it rejects the reality of UFOs simply because the government has made it unfashionable to believe otherwise. As a matter of fact, the government appears to count heavily on this human weakness to maintain a mythical status to the situation. Under that condition, virtually any mundane alternative that comes to mind makes an acceptable answer. Of course, it doesn't hurt to provide a little help. . .

Kevin Randle describes how the balloon, which was used to explain away the famous 1947 Roswell incident, was misused a number of times elsewhere, citing the case of an interview with a former Air Force sergeant in which the man admitted to falsely creating everyday answers for sighting events. These were made under orders from above with the purpose of calming the civilians and preventing the sightings from reaching news outlets. One of the sergeant's favorite ploys was to pin the cause on Navy Skyhook balloons rather than UFOs. The balloons actually were used, but not at the time or the area of the sightings, according to the sergeant. When pressed in the interview with repeated questions designed to explicitly verify the man's account, the investigator was reassured that the sergeant had indeed given false information to the press upon orders from the Pentagon. Those who participated in the disinformation claimed to have been scared of retribution if they didn't obey the Pentagon- initiated directives.

The Roswell incident was included in this misinformation campaign. For an account of the Roswell incident, please refer to Report #1 of Chapter Twenty Two above.

Looking back over the decades between the '50s and the new millennium, one can see so much obvious evidence of government/media manipulation of the public in other areas that the idea of governmental intervention in the area of UFO sightings is rather easy to digest. Racial bigotry in America is becoming a thing of the past. So is the stigma against what used to be considered sexual misconduct, religious intolerance (except against fundamental Christians), cigarette smoking, personal privacy, the right to bear arms for self-protection, and the cash transaction. Children are less frequently abused, but instead have become the abusers of parents and authority figures. Same-sex marriage is no longer frowned upon. The search for personal excellence has been replaced by the quest for cheap fun. This change has taken place in an astonishingly short time, much too short to have occurred naturally.

Whether the several social engineering projects that have created this new society may have been motivated by perceived necessity or even noble ideals is not the issue. The attempts have been made, the efforts themselves represent an unconscionable arrogance, and if one ignores the side effects, they have been spectacularly successful to date. If one stops to think about it, it is startling to perceive how narrow the range of acceptable thought has become.

The point of this digression is that the very activity of the government in attempting to modify public behavior regarding UFO sightings of itself makes a strong case for their ultimate reality.

The UFO researchers and authors who have focused on the historic side of the alien thesis have also been subjected to a substantial amount of media sensationalism and debunking. These writers have offered variants of the basic theme of alien visitations in our ancient past that exhibit more agreement among them than differences. In presenting their conclusions, these authors refer to enigmatic, often strangely technical, accounts pointing to alien visitors found in the ancient and sacred writings and traditions of a variety of societies, including the Hebrew Torah and prophetic writings, Old Testament episodes, extrabiblical writings of the Hebrews, the Vedas of the Hindus, Egyptian structures and hieroglyphics, the annals of the

Central and South American Indians, and the more recently-deciphered texts of the ancient Sumerians.

Their primary detractors are the mainstream archaeologists who represent the established universities. Sometimes the writers of the historic alien genre have played right into the hands of the sensationalists, but for the most part they have been victims of the rigidity and politicization of standard science, which, like any entrenched institution, is encumbered by its own bureaucracy and bureaucratic way of thinking.

Nevertheless, the mainstream sciences have failed to explain the numerous puzzles of our past which so thoroughly contradict the notion that mankind's acquisition of knowledge has been steadily and unidirectionally increasing from the stone age to the present without the benefit of assistance from some other species beyond our own.

In the light of the accounts presented above, one can readily discern the importance of independent thought. The popularity of a prevailing paradigm regarding a subject is not a measure of its truth.

PART SEVEN

HINTS OF GOD

CHAPTER TWENTY FOUR

UFO or God – or Both?

My own UFO experience, given the knowledge I had acquired of Scripture and the basic nature of God, as well as the physical and mental activities associated with Christian service, certainly qualifies as involving God, and in a manner significantly more profound than merely hinting of such.

My personal experience is also reminiscent of an event cited in Jacques Vallee's *Dimensions*. In fact, the two events are almost identical, particularly in the aftermath of the sightings. In that particular event, which took place in the summer of 1968, the female witness was driving from London to the vicinity of Stratford with a companion to visit friends. Their sighting began outside Oxford, where they saw a shining disc that darted about in the sky. They stopped the car to watch it, along with another car that also had stopped. They continued on their way after the UFO sank behind some trees.

That wasn't the end of the story. The important element of the sighting was the aftermath. According to the witness, she had experienced novel insights into what she described as the nature of reality during the drive between Burford and Stratford. To her, this understanding, which she connected to the UFO, was not only startling but effected her so profoundly as to cause a personality change and convert her from agnosticism to what she called Gnosticism. Her new understanding transcended what the various religions of the world attempted to claim about God. The experience happened just once, not to be repeated with her.

As noted above, this report has much in common with my own:

It was a multiple-witness sighting.

The UFO was disc-shaped, and performed what may be considered common maneuvers. It 'sank behind the trees' after the observation.

The sighting was apparently only of the first kind, but in which the UFO occupants had the ability to communicate telepathically with the witness. Perhaps the main witness may have realized an unexplained time lapse at a later date.

This sighting may be considered to be a positive experience, at least by the witness. The most important event to the witness took place after the sighting. The experience had religious connotations; in both cases the primary witnesses were not previously religious. It was a life-changing event.

Many experiences like these, while extra-Biblical, are related to our Judeo-Christian God. The more modern events, of course, have occurred in time beyond the canonization of Scripture; nevertheless, they are reminiscent of events described by Scripture itself, as will be explored in a following chapter. While some might consider these "outside" events to signify a source other than God, it is more reasonable to expect that God has continued to interact with the human race since the canonization of Scripture than to believe His interaction ceased after Scripture was completed.

These extra-Biblical UFO experiences have been overtly religious and can be interpreted as being either positive or negative according to the investigator's point of view. Many of these experiences also are informationally rich, indicating their truthfulness.

One such famous incident occurred in 1917 in Fatima, Portugal. In that event, the apparition of a lady appeared to three children. Two of the children subsequently died in the great influenza epidemic following World War 1, supposedly with the full knowledge of and joyful anticipation of their coming death. The third, Lucia, lived to the age of 97, passing away in 2005. The children were given three secrets by the apparition, interpreted as Mary by the Catholic Church. The first involved a vision of hell. The second involved a request to save souls and a command to consecrate Russia to Mary, with the warning that if Russia didn't return to God, another, worse war would occur during the tenure of Pope Pius XI. This prophecy was fulfilled in 1939, the year that Pope Pius XI died.

There is an element of cloak-and-dagger regarding the third secret of Fatima. Lucia had cautioned that it was not to be revealed until 1960, but the Catholic Church continued to hold it secret until 2000, when the secret was declared to have been a vision of a Pope climbing up a hill toward a cross, accompanied by many Church leaders and other Christians. Upon reaching the cross at the summit, they were gunned down by soldiers. Angels were said to have collected their shed blood. But there is still controversy regarding this third secret, with many claiming that the third mystery revealed more than the Church has been willing to disclose. At any rate, Popes Pius XII, Paul VI, John Paul II and Benedict XVI have all strongly acknowledged their acceptance of the Fatima apparition and the secrets as supernatural fact. In 2010 Pope Benedict XVI repeated this conviction. Other apparitions of Mary have been witnessed, including eighteen appearances to Bernadette Soubirous at Lourdes, France, and a number of events at Medjugorje, Bosnia beginning in June, 1981.

The well-known Fatima miracle, as popular UFO researcher Jacques Vallee relates, was connected with UFOs. According to him, the Fatima case provides an example of the connection between UFO encounters and religion. Two years before the famous Fatima incident, the area experienced a series of classical UFO sightings. As interpreted by the Catholic Church, the Fatima event was unexplainable in purely physical terms, and illusion also was taken off the table after thirteen years of detailed investigation. The Church stated that:

"'The solar phenomenon of the 13th of October 1917, described in the press of the time, was most marvelous and caused the greatest impression on those who had the happiness of witnessing it. . .

"'This phenomenon, which no astronomical observatory registered and which therefore was not natural, was witnessed by persons of all categories and of all social classes, believers and unbelievers, journalists of the principal Portuguese newspapers and even by persons some miles away. Facts which annul any explanation of collective illusion.'"

The Fatima incident also had been predicted months earlier by three children who had a vision of a brightly glowing woman. Most interestingly supportive to my view of the Holy Spirit is that this "woman" had never told them that she was the Virgin Mary. Having been brought up Catholic, the children simply assumed that. Instead, the woman told them that she came from Heaven. She told them to return there every month until October, when a miracle would take place in front of the public to the end that they all might believe.

The Fatima apparitions included luminous spheres and falling-leaf maneuvers, odd-colored lights and heat, which are associated with some classic UFO events. Psychic events often associated with UFO sightings, such as prophecy and loss of consciousness, also occurred.

Vallee goes on to describe various messages given to selected individuals, the prophetic statements, and the several follow-on apparitions that comprise the Fatima miracle. He notes features of the events, like buzzing sounds experienced by some witnesses, which are characteristic of modern UFO sightings. Some prophesies are quite specific, as noted by Vallee, such as the warning that although the war (World War I) would end, unless people stop offending God another worse one would begin during the reign of Pope Pius XI. The Pope died in 1939, years after the prophecy and indeed at the beginning of World War II. She told them that when they see a night illuminated by an unknown light they should know that this would be the sign that God is giving them that He is going to punish the world for its crimes by means of war, famine, and persecution of the Church. She told them that she would come to ask for the consecration of Russia. If her pleas would be heeded, Russia would be converted and there would be peace instead of war. Otherwise, Russia will spread her errors throughout the world.

Vallee then makes a curious statement regarding this prophecy, noting that it, like the sighting at Lourdes, contains a mixture of seriousness and absurdity, which are unmistakable characteristics of UFO contactee stories.

Did the statement have absurd elements? As time marches on, these apparent absurdities become clarified. World War II began the same year Pius XI died. Major events which precipitated it occurred during his reign. According to Christian (and Western) thought, Russia has indeed spread her errors throughout the world.

Perhaps the absurdities, if any, are perceived out of an incomplete grasp of the event, or of the intimate relationship between a given event and others that might not seem connected at the time. Vallee himself quoted Hartland in his *Science of Fairy Tales* to the effect that in fairy transactions the fairly commonplace gift of an apparently worthless object ends up to be of the utmost value. Hartland perceived that to be an obvious manifestation of superhuman power.

Elements of the tale which evoked that response involve another beautiful representation of Mary in Catholic lore. In this historic incident that took place just outside Mexico City in the year 1531 a Mexican peasant named Juan Diego visited his dying uncle in an effort to comfort him. In that tale, as also related by Father John Macquarrie in his book *Mary for all Christians*, an apparition of who he assumed to be Mary appeared to the peasant. At the time, Juan's uncle was very ill, to the point of near-death. He spent a day trying to relieve his uncle's sufferings and left him only on

Tuesday, to get a priest. An apparition of Mary barred his way. She told him not to be afraid, informing him that She was his (Holy) Mother under Her shadow and protection. She told Juan that her uncle would not die, but even now was being restored. She gave him another errand, telling him to go to the top of the nearby hill, cut the flowers that were growing there, and bring them to Her. As it was winter, Juan expected to see no flowers. But when he came to the top of the hill, he found Castilian Roses growing there. He cut them and brought them back to the Woman, who carefully arranged the flowers in Juan's crudely-woven cape and then tied the corners of the cape behind his neck. She instructed him to let only the bishop see what she had done.

Meanwhile, the room where Juan's uncle awaited the priest was filled with light, and a luminous young woman appeared before him. He was indeed cured.

When Juan reached the bishop's palace several servants made sport of him, pushing him around and trying to snatch the flowers from his cape. But the flowers dissolved when they reached for them. Amazed, they let him go. When he reached the bishop, Juan Diego untied the corners of the cape and as the ends dropped the flowers fell out in a jumbled heap. The disappointed peasant became confused as to the purpose of his visit. But then he was astonished to see that the bishop had come over to him and was kneeling at his feet. Soon everyone else in the room had come near and they all were kneeling with the bishop.

Juan Diego's cape now hangs over the altar in the basilica of Our Lady of Guadalupe in Mexico City. Over eight million persons were baptized there in the six years that followed this event. Many millions more since that time have knelt before the two-piece cape, coarsely-woven of maguey fibers, for imprinted on it is an intricately detailed, beautiful figure of Mary. In her graceful posture she appears kind and lovable. She is surrounded by golden rays. Fifteen hundred persons a day still visit the shrine. The image is available on the Internet by Googling on "Juan Diego".

Some items of interesting information have emerged recently regarding Our Lady of Guadalupe, as the Catholic Church has named this apparition. She apparently never identified Herself to Juan Diego as Mary, but rather as Juan Diego's Mother. Second, Her image, as can be seen by Googling Juan Diego, matches that of the Aztec goddess. Third, according to a theologian in the La Ermita community in Macon, Georgia, the indigenous converts to Christianity, in opposition to the Catholic insistence on perceiving the apparition as Mary, refused to worship Her as such and insisted upon worshiping Her as God. To a Christian who perceives the Holy Spirit as feminine, this would make perfect sense.

The same type of apparition has occurred more recently with messages from a spiritual being whom the Catholic Church also associates with Mary. In fact, some messages from this lady have been very recent. The apparition first appeared at Medjugorje, Bosnia-Herzegovina on June 24, 1981, with the urgent mission of asserting to the world that God truly exists, and that path to joy and peace requires man to return to Him. Her message has in the past and continues to be given to six people residing in Herzegovina: Ivan, Jakov, Marija, Mirjana, Vicka, and Ivanka. In her daily appearance to them, this lady gives the six visionaries public messages and private 'secrets'. There will be ten 'secrets' in all, after which the lady will stop appearing to the visionaries on a daily basis, but will reappear one day each year for the rest of their lives. To date, Mirjana, Jakov and Ivanka have each received their ten 'secrets', and Marija, Vicka and Ivan have each received nine.

The Medjugorje.org Website includes a cryptic and unsettling paragraph that reads:

"Once Our Lady has stopped appearing there will be three warnings given to the world. These warnings will be in the form of events on earth. They will occur within Mirjana's lifetime, and Mirjana will be a witness to them. Ten days before each of the warnings, she will advise the priest she chose for this task (Father Petar Ljubicic), who will then pray and fast with Mirjana for seven days. Then, three days before each warning is to take place, Fr. Petar will announce to the world what, where, and when the warning will take place. Fr. Petar has no choice, and must reveal each warning. After the first warning, the other two will follow in a rather short period of time. That interval will be a period of great grace and conversion. After the permanent, visible, supernatural, and indestructible sign appears on the mountain where Our Lady first appeared in Medjugorje, there will be little time for conversion. For that reason, the Blessed Virgin invites us to urgent conversion and reconciliation. The permanent sign will lead to many healings and conversions before the secrets become reality. According to Mirjana, the events predicted by the Blessed Virgin are near. By virtue of this experience, Mirjana proclaims to the world: 'Hurry, be converted; open your hearts to God.'"

The "permanent sign" spoken in the paragraph above was to be the third secret, in which the woman has promised to leave a supernatural and permanent sign on the mountain where she first appeared. The sign was to be intended for the atheists. She cautioned all the faithful to deepen their faith and truly convert soon as the present time was a time of grace for them. She finished with the ominous statement that when the sign does come, it will be too late for many.

Chapter Twenty Five

UFO Activity in Scripture

The Bible is replete with accounts that in a modern context would surely be attributed to UFOs. Most of these accounts are far from demonic. Instead they reflect the will of God as it is presented in Scripture.

It is an indisputable fact that the Bible contains numerous accounts of the appearance of God or His angelic representatives to man, and even of the direct intervention of God into the affairs of mankind. Because of their otherworldly nature, we might rightly call many of these events UFO experiences. Several of the more well-known examples are given below:

Example 1 - Genesis 6:1-4:

> *"And it came to pass, when men began to multiply on the face of the earth, and daughters were born unto them, that the sons of God saw the daughters of men that they were fair; and they took them wives of all whom they chose.*

> *"And the Lord said, My Spirit shall not always strive with man, for that he also is flesh: yet his days shall be an hundred and twenty years.*

> *"There were giants in the earth in those days; and also after that, when the sons of God came in unto the daughters of men, and they bore children unto them, the same became mighty men who were of old, men of renown."*

Example 2 - Genesis 14:18-20:

"And Melchizedek, king of Salem, brought forth bread and wine; and he was the priest of the most high God. And he blessed him, and said, Blessed be Abram of the most high God, possessor of heaven and earth: and blessed be the most high God, who hath delivered thine enemies into thy hand. And he gave him tithes of all."

Example 3 - Genesis 18:1-5, 16-23, 19:15-17:

"And the Lord appeared unto [Abraham] in the plains of Mamre: and he sat in the tent door in the heat of the day; And he lifted up his eyes and looked, and, lo, three men stood by him: and when he saw them, he ran to meet them from the tent door, and bowed himself toward the ground, And said, My Lord, if now I have found favor in thy sight, pass not away, I pray thee, from thy servant: Let a little water, I pray you, be fetched, and wash your feet, and rest yourselves under the tree: And I will fetch a morsel of bread, and comfort ye your hearts; after that ye shall pass on: for therefore are ye come to your servant. And they said, So do, as thou hast said."

"And the men rose up from thence, and looked toward Sodom: and Abraham went with them to bring them on the way. And the Lord said, Shall I hide from Abraham that thing which I do; Seeing that Abraham shall become a great and mighty nation, and all the nations shall be blessed in him? For I know him, that he will command his children and his household after him, and they shall keep the way of the Lord, to do justice and judgment; that the Lord may bring upon Abraham that which he hath spoken of him.

"And the Lord said, Because the cry of Sodom and Gomorrah is great, and because their sin is very grievous, I will go down now, and see whether they have done altogether according to the cry of it, which is come unto me; and if not, I will know.

"And the men turned their faces from thence, and went toward Sodom: but Abraham stood yet before the Lord.

"And Abraham drew near, and said, Wilt thou also destroy the righteous with the wicked?"

"And when the morning arose, then the angels hastened Lot, saying, Arise, take thy wife, and thy two daughters, which are here; lest thou

be consumed in the iniquity of the city. And while he lingered, the men laid hold upon his hand, and upon the hand of his wife, and upon the hand of his two daughters; the Lord being merciful unto him: and they brought him forth, and set him without the city.

"And it came to pass, when they brought them forth abroad, that he said, Escape for thy life; look not behind thee, neither stay thou in all the plain; escape to the mountain, lest thou be consumed."

This account does not mention how the men first appeared to Abraham. They could have appeared suddenly, simply walked into sight, or have arrived in a craft before or at the time Abraham sighted them. There is every indication, on the other hand, that Abraham knew that these 'men' were extraordinary from the beginning. That he perceived them to have unusual powers is beyond dispute. Their display of power in destroying Sodom is obvious, as is the purpose behind their appearance. The full Biblical account gives them prophetic power as well in predicting Sarah's ability to bear a child in her old age. There is some correspondence between this event and modern 'apparitions', such as the Fatima sighting.

Example 4 – Genesis 28:12-22:

"And [Jacob] dreamed, and behold a ladder set up on the earth, and the top of it reached to heaven: and behold the angels of God ascending and descending on it. And, behold, the Lord stood above it, and said, I am the Lord God of Abraham, thy father, and the God of Isaac: the land whereon thou liest, to thee will I give it, and to thy seed; and thy seed shall be as the dust of the earth, and thou shalt spread abroad to the west, and to the east, and to the north, and to the south; and in thee and in thy seed shall all the families of the earth be blessed. And, behold, I am with thee, and will keep thee in all places to which thou goest, and will bring thee again unto this land; for I will not leave thee, until I have done that which I have spoken to thee of. And Jacob awaked out of his sleep, and he said, Surely the Lord is in this place; and I knew it not. And he was afraid, and said, How awesome is this place! This is none other than the house of God, and this is the gate of heaven.

"And Jacob rose up early in the morning, and took the stone that he had put for his pillows, and set it up for a pillar, and poured oil upon the top of it. And he called the name of that place Bethel: but the name of that city was called Luz at the first. And Jacob vowed a vow,

saying If God will be with me, and will keep me in this way that I go, and will give me bread to eat, and raiment to put on, so that I come again to my father's house in peace; then shall the Lord be my God: and this stone, which I have set for a pillar, shall be God's house: and of all that thou shalt give me I will surely give the tenth unto thee."

Example 5 – Genesis 32:24-32:

"And Jacob was left alone; and there wrestled a man with him until the breaking of the day. And when he saw that he prevailed not against him, he touched the hollow of his thigh; and the hollow of Jacob's thigh was out of joint, as he wrestled against him. And he said, Let me go; for the day breaketh. And he said, I will not let thee go, except thou bless me. And he said unto him, What is thy name? And he said, Jacob. And he said, Thy name shall be called no more Jacob, but Israel; for as a prince hast thou power with God and with men, and hast prevailed. And Jacob asked him, and said, Tell me, I pray thee, thy name. And he said, Wherefore is it that thou dost ask after my name? And he blessed him there.

"And Jacob called the place Peniel; for I have seen God face to face, and my life is preserved. And as he passed over Penuel the sun rose upon him, and he limped upon his thigh. Therefore the children of Israel eat not of the sinew which shrank, which is upon the hollow of the thigh, unto this day: because he touched the hollow of Jacob's thigh in the sinew that shrank."

Example 6 - Exodus 3:1-14, 4:1-5:

"Now Moses kept the flock of Jethro his father-in-law, the priest of Midian: and he led the flock to the back side of the desert, and came to the mountain of God, even to Horeb.

"And the Angel of the Lord appeared unto him in a flame of fire out of the midst of a bush: and he looked, and, behold, the bush burned with fire, and the bush was not consumed.

"And Moses said, I will now turn aside, and see this great sight, why the bush is not burnt. And when the Lord saw that he turned aside to see, God called unto him out of the midst of the bush, and said, Moses, Moses. And he said, Here am I.

"And he said, Draw not nigh hither: put off thy shoes from off thy feet; for the place whereon thou standest is holy ground. Moreover he said, I am the God of thy father, the God of Abraham, the God of Isaac, and the God of Jacob. And Moses hid his face; for he was afraid to look upon God.

"And the Lord said, I have surely seen the affliction of my people which are in Egypt, and have heard their cry by reason of their taskmasters; for I know their sorrows; And I am come down to deliver them out of the hand of the Egyptians, and to bring them up out of that land unto a good land and a large, unto a land flowing with milk and honey; unto the place of the Canaanites, and the Hittites, and the Amorites, and the Perizzites, and the Hivites, and the Jebusites.

"Now therefore, behold, the cry of the children of Israel is come unto me: and I have also seen the oppression wherewith the Egyptians oppress them. Come now therefore, and I will send thee unto Pharaoh, that thou mayest bring forth my people the children of Israel out of Egypt.

"And Moses said unto God, Who am I, that I should go unto Pharaoh, and that I should bring forth the children of Israel out of Egypt?

"And he said, Certainly I will be with thee; and this shall be a token unto thee, that I have sent thee: When thou hast brought forth the people out of Egypt, ye shall serve God upon this mountain.

"And Moses said unto God, Behold, when I come unto the children of Israel, and shall say unto them, The God of your fathers hath sent me unto you; and they shall say to me, What is his name? what shall I say unto them?

"And God said unto Moses, I AM THAT I AM: and he said: Thus shalt thou say unto the children of Israel, I AM hath sent me unto you."

"And Moses answered and said, But, behold, they will not believe me, nor hearken unto my voice: for they will say, The Lord hath not appeared unto thee.

"And the Lord said unto him, What is that in thine hand? And he said, A rod. And he said, Cast it on the ground. And he cast it on the ground, and it became a serpent; and Moses fled from before it.

"And the Lord said unto Moses, Put forth thine hand, and take it by the tail. And he put forth his hand, and caught it, and it became a rod in his hand: That they may believe that the Lord God of their fathers, the God of Abraham, the God of Isaac, and the God of Jacob, hath appeared unto thee."

The much more recent apparition which appeared to Juan Diego in the sixteenth century, and to the peasant girls in Fatima in the twentieth century, recounted in an earlier chapter, may not have been as significant as this appearance before Moses. But they did contain some of the same elements, such as commandments to appear before powerful individuals, and the empowerment to produce remarkable signs.

Example 7 – Exodus 40:34-38:

"Then a cloud covered the tent of the congregation, and the glory of the Lord filled the tabernacle. And Moses was not able to enter into the tent of the congregation, because the cloud abode thereon, and the glory of the Lord filled the tabernacle.

"And when the cloud was taken up from over the tabernacle, the children of Israel went onward in all their journeys; but if the cloud were not taken up, then they journeyed not till the day that it was taken up. For the cloud of the Lord was upon the tabernacle by day, and fire was on it by night, in the sight of all the house of Israel, throughout all their journeys."

This event occurred again when Solomon dedicated the first temple, as recorded in 1 Kings 8:10-13:

"And it came to pass, when the priests were come out of the holy place, that the cloud filled the house of the Lord, so that the priests could not stand to minister because of the cloud; for the glory of the Lord had filled the house of the Lord.

"Then spoke Solomon, The Lord said that he would dwell in the thick darkness. I have surely built thee an house to dwell in, a settled place for thee to abide in forever."

These events of the temple indwellings have a special significance to me, as I view them as foreshadowing the indwelling of the Holy Spirit to Christians in the Upper Room as described in Acts 2 and explained by Paul in 1 Corinthians 3:16 and Ephesians 2:19-22. This significance increases as the indwelling Hebrew *Shekinah* is acknowledged to have a feminine gender.

Example 8 - Joshua 1:1-11:

"Now after the death of Moses the servant of the Lord, it came to pass, that the Lord spake unto Joshua the son of Nun, Moses' minister, saying, Moses my servant is dead; now therefore arise, go over this Jordan, thou, and all this people, unto the land which I do give to them, even to the children of Israel.

"Every place that the sole of your foot shall tread upon, that have I given unto you, as I said unto Moses. From the wilderness and this Lebanon even unto the great river, the river Euphrates, all the land of the Hittites, and unto the great sea toward the going down of the sun, shall be your coast.

"There shall not any man be able to stand before thee all the days of thy life: as I was with Moses, so I will be with thee: I will not fail thee, nor forsake thee.

"Be strong and of a good courage: for unto this people shalt thou divide for and inheritance the land, which I sware unto their fathers to give them. Only be thou strong and very courageous, that thou mayest observe to do according to all the law, which Moses my servant commanded thee: turn no from it to the right hand or to the left, that thou mayest prosper whithersoever thou goest.

"This book of the law shall not depart out of thy mouth; but thou shalt meditate therein day and night, that thou mayest observe to do according to all that is written therein: for then thou shalt make thy way prosperous, and then thou shalt have good success.

"Have I not commanded thee? Be strong and of a good courage; be not afraid, neither be thou dismayed: for the Lord thy God is with thee whithersoever thou goest.

"Then Joshua commanded the officers of the people, saying, Pass through the host, and command the people, saying, Prepare you victuals; for within three days ye shall pass over this Jordan, to go in to possess the land, which the Lord your God giveth you to possess it."

Example 9 - Joshua 5:13-15:

"And it came to pass, when Joshua was by Jericho, that he lifted up his eyes and looked, and, behold, there stood a man over against him with his sword drawn in his hand: and Joshua went unto him, and said unto him, Art thou for us, or for our adversaries?

"And he sad, Nay; but as captain of the host of the Lord am I now come. And Joshua fell on his face to the earth, and did worship, and said unto him, What saith my lord unto his servant?

"And the captain of the Lord's host said unto Joshua, Loose thy shoe from off thy foot; for the place whereon thou standest is holy. And Joshua did so.

Example 10 - Joshua 6:2-5, 15,16,20:

"And the Lord said unto Joshua, See, I have given into thy hand Jericho, and the king thereof, and the mighty men of valor. And ye shall compass the city, all ye men of war, and go round about the city once. Thus shalt thou do six days. And seven priests shall bear before the ark seven trumpets of rams' horns: and the seventh day ye shall compass the city seven times, and the priests shall blow with the trumpets. And it shall come to pass, that when they make a long blast with the ram's horn, and when ye hear the sound of the trumpet, all the people shall shout with a great shout; and the wall of the city shall fall down flat, and the people shall ascend up every man straight before him."

"And it came to pass on the seventh day, that they rose early about the dawning of the day, and compassed the city after the same manner seven times: only on that day they compassed the city seven times. And it came to pass at the seventh time, when the priests blew with the trumpets, Joshua said unto the people, Shout; for the Lord hath given you the city."

"So the people shouted when the priests blew with the trumpets: and it came to pass, when the people heard the sound of the trumpet, and the people shouted with a great shout, that the wall fell down flat, so that the people went up into the city, every man straight before him, and they took the city."

As in the case with Moses before him, Joshua's adventures were accompanied with signs and miracles. Also as with Moses, his adventures were preceded by the sighting of an apparition, who commanded him to display courage.

Example 11 - 2 Kings 2:1-13:

"And it came to pass, when the Lord would take up Elijah into heaven by a whirlwind, that Elijah went with Elisha from Gilgal. And Elijah said unto Elisha, Tarry here, I pray thee; for the Lord hath sent me to Bethel. And Elisha said unto him, As the Lord liveth, and as thy soul liveth, I will not leave thee. So they went down to Bethel. And the sons of the prophets that were at Bethel came forth to Elisha, and said unto him, Knowest thou that the Lord will take away thy master from thy head today? And he said, Yea, I know it; hold ye your peace.

"And Elijah said unto him, Tarry, I pray thee, here; for the Lord hath sent me to Jordan. And he said, As the Lord liveth, and as thy soul liveth, I will not leave thee. And they two went on. And fifty men of the sons of the prophets went, and stood to view afar off: and they two stood by Jordan.

"And Elijah took his mantle, and wrapped it together, and smote the waters, and they were divided hither and thither, so that they two went over on dry ground.

"And it came to pass, when they were gone over, that Elijah said unto Elisha, Ask what I shall do for thee, before I shall be taken away from thee. And Elisha said, I pray thee, let a double portion of thy spirit be upon me. And he said, thou hast asked a hard thing: nevertheless, if thou see me when I am taken from thee, it shall be so unto thee; but if not, it shall not be so.

"And it came to pass, as they still went on, and talked, that, behold, there appeared a chariot of fire, and horses of fire, and parted them both asunder; and Elijah went up by a whirlwind into heaven.

"And Elisha saw it, and he cried, My father, my father, the chariot of Israel, and the horsemen thereof! And he saw him no more: and he took hold of his own clothes, and rent them in two pieces. He took up also the mantle of Elijah that fell from him, and went back, and stood by the bank of Jordan."

Here is what we would call a classic UFO abduction case, complete with the UFO itself. Did this encounter affect Elisha thereafter? We see the answer in 2 Kings 2:14, 15:

> "And he took the mantle of Elijah that fell from him, and smote the waters, and said, Where is the Lord God of Elijah? And when he also had smitten the waters, they parted hither and thither: and Elisha went over.

> "And when the sons of the prophets which were to view at Jericho saw him, they said, The spirit of Elijah doth rest on Elisha. And they came to meet him, and bowed themselves to the ground before him.

Example 12 - Ezekiel 1:1-28:

> "Now it came to pass in the thirtieth year, in the fourth month, in the fifth day of the month, as I was among the captives by the river of Chebar, that the heavens were opened, and I saw visions of God. In the fifth day of the month, which was the fifth year of king Jehoiachin's captivity, The word of the Lord came expressly unto Ezekiel the priest, the son of Buzi, in the land of the Chaldeans by the river Chebar; and the hand of the Lord was there upon him.

> "And I looked, and, behold, a whirlwind came out of the north, a great cloud, and a fire infolding itself, and a brightness was about it, and out of the midst thereof as the color of amber, out of the midst of the fire. Also out of the midst thereof came the likeness of four living creatures. And this was their appearance; they had the likeness of a man. And every one had four faces, and every one had four wings. And their feet were straight feet; and the sole of their feet was like the sole of a calf's foot: and they sparkled like the color of burnished brass. And they had the hands of a man under their wings on their four sides; and they four had their faces and their wings. Their wings were joined one to another; they turned not when they went; they went every one straight forward. As for the likeness of their faces, they four had the face of a man, and the face of a lion, on the right side: and they four had the face of an ox on the left side; they four also had the face of an eagle. Thus were their faces; and their wings were stretched upward; two wings of every one were joined one to another, and two covered their bodies. And they went every one straight forward: whither the spirit was to go, they went; and they turned not when they

went. As for the likeness of the living creatures, their appearance was like burning coals of fire, and like the appearance of lamps: it went up and down among the living creatures; and the fire was bright, and out of the fire went forth lightning. And the living creatures ran and returned as the appearance of a flash of lightning.

"Now as I beheld the living creatures, behold one wheel upon the earth by the living creatures, with his four faces. The appearance of the wheels and their work was like unto the color of beryl: and they four had one likeness: and their appearance and their work was as it were a wheel in the middle of a wheel. When they went, they went upon their four sides: and they turned not when they went. As for their rings, they were so high that they were dreadful; and their rings were full of eyes round about them four. And when the living creatures went, the wheels went by them: and when the living creatures were lifted up from the earth, the wheels were lifted up. Whithersoever the spirit was to go, they went, thither was their spirit to go; and the wheels were lifted up over against them: for the spirit of the living creature was in the wheels.

"And the likeness of the firmament upon the heads of the living creature was as the color of the terrible crystal, stretched forth over their heads above. And under the firmament were their wings straight, the one toward the other: every one had two, which covered on this side, and every one had two, which covered on that side, their bodies.

"And when they went, I heard the noise of their wings, like the noise of great waters, as the voice of the Almighty, the voice of speech, as the noise of a host: when they stood, they let down their wings. And there was a voice from the firmament that was over their heads, when they stood, and had let down their wings.

"And above the firmament that was over their heads was the likeness of a throne, as the appearance of a sapphire stone: and upon the likeness of the throne was the likeness as the appearance of a man above upon it. And I saw as the color of amber, as the appearance of fire round about within it, from the appearance of his loins even upward, and from the appearance of his loins even downward, I saw as it were the appearance of fire, and it had brightness round about. As the appearance of the bow that is in the cloud in the day of rain, so was the appearance of the brightness round about. This was the

appearance of the likeness of the glory of the Lord. And when I saw it, I fell upon my face, and I heard a voice of one that spake."

This event has been thoroughly revisited by modern writers, who note the obvious correspondence with recent UFO sightings. Here again, as in modern sightings with a religious flavor, the sighting had a long-term impact on the witness. There is abundant evidence in the chapters in Ezekiel that follow that great prophetic wisdom was imparted to Ezekiel. His life was changed forever as he followed the prophetic command noted below.

Example 13 - Ezekiel 2:1-3:

"And he said unto me, Son of man, stand upon thy feet, and I will speak unto thee. And the spirit entered into me when he spake unto me, and set me upon my feet, that I heard him that spake unto me. And he said unto me, Son of man, I send thee to the children of Israel, to a rebellious nation that hath rebelled against me: they and their fathers have transgressed, against me, even unto this very day."

The late Bible scholar Grant Jeffrey extracted from God's commandment in Ezekiel 4 to lie on his left side for three hundred ninety days for the iniquity of Israel and on his right side for forty days for the iniquity of Judah, coupled with the extended duration noted in Leviticus 26, the exact date of May 14, 1948 for the return of Israel as a nation. Details of this amazing prophecy are given in my novel *Cathy*. Moreover, a great many present-day Jews and Christians consider Ezekiel's 'dry bones' prophecy in the 36th chapter to have had a remarkably accurate fulfillment in the restoration of the State of Israel following the Holocaust in World War II.

Example 14 - Daniel 10:5-21, 12:1-13:

"Then I lifted up mine eyes, and looked, and behold a certain man clothed in linen, whose loins were girded with fine gold of Uphaz: His body also was like the beryl, and his face as the appearance of lightning, and his eyes as lamps of fire, and his arms and his feet like in color to polished brass, and the voice of his words like the voice of a multitude.

"And I Daniel alone saw the vision: for the men that were with me saw not the vision; but a great quaking fell upon them, so that they fled to hide themselves. Therefore I was left alone, and saw this great vision, and there remained no strength in me: for my

comeliness was turned into corruption, and I retained no strength. Yet heard I the voice of his words: and when I heard the voice of his words, then was I in a deep sleep on my face, and my face toward the ground.

"And, behold, a hand touched me, which set me upon my knees and upon the palms of my hands. And he said unto me, O Daniel, a man greatly beloved, understand the words that I speak unto thee, and stand upright: for unto thee am I now sent. And when he had spoken this word unto me, I stood trembling.

"Then said he unto me, Fear not, Daniel; for from the first day that thou didst set thine heart to understand, and to chasten thyself before thy God, thy words were heard, and I am come for thy words. But the prince of Persia withstood me for one and twenty days; but, lo, Michael, one of the chief princes, came to help me; and I remained there with the kings of Persia.

"Now I am come to make thee understand what shall befall thy people in the latter days: for yet the visions is for many days.

"And when he had spoken such words unto me, I set my face toward the ground, and I became dumb. And, behold, one like the similitude of the sons of men touched my lips: then I opened my mouth, and spake, and said unto him that stood before me, O my lord, by the vision my sorrows are turned upon me, and I have retained no strength. For how can the servant of this my lord talk with this my lord? For as for me, straightway there remained no strength in me, neither is there breath left in me.

"Then there came again and touched me one like the appearance of a man, and he strengthened me, And said, O man greatly beloved, fear not: peace be unto thee; be strong, yea, be strong. And when he had spoken unto me, I was strengthened, and said, Let my lord speak; for thou hast strengthened me.

"Then said he, Knowest thou wherefore I come unto thee? and now will I return to fight with the prince of Persia: and when I am gone forth, lo, the prince of Grecia shall come. But I will show thee that which is noted in the Scripture of truth: and there is none that holdeth with me in these things, but Michael your prince."

"And at that time shall Michael stand up, the great prince which standeth for the children of thy people: and there shall be a time of trouble, such as never was since there was a nation even to that same time: and at that time thy people shall be delivered, every one that shall be found written in the book. And many of them that sleep in the dust of the earth shall, awake, some to everlasting life, and some to shame and everlasting contempt. And they that be wise shall shine as the brightness of the firmament; and they that turn many to righteousness, as the stars for ever and ever.

"But thou, O Daniel, shut up the words, and seal the book, even to the time of the end: many shall run to and fro, and knowledge shall be increased.

"Then I Daniel looked, and, behold, there stood other two, the one on this side of the bank of the river, and the other on that side of the bank of the river. And one said to the man clothed in linen, which was upon the waters of the river, How long shall it be to the end of these wonders? And I heard the man clothed in linen, which was upon the waters of the river, when he held up his right hand and his left hand unto heaven, and sware by him that liveth for ever, that it shall be for a time, times, and a half; and when he shall have accomplished to scatter the power of the holy people, all these things shall be finished.

"And I heard, but I understood not: then said I, O my Lord, what shall be the end of these things?

"And he said, Go thy way, Daniel: for the words are closed up and sealed till the time of the end. Many shall be purified, and made white, and tried; but the wicked shall do wickedly: and none of the wicked shall understand; but the wise shall understand. And from the time that the daily sacrifice shall be taken away, and the abomination that maketh desolate set up, there shall be a thousand two hundred and ninety days. Blessed is he that waiteth, and cometh to the thousand three hundred and five and thirty days.

"But go thy way till the end be: for thou shalt rest, and stand in thy lot at the end of the days."

The 'angel' who appeared to Daniel would be treated as a 'Close Encounter of the Third Kind' today. These passages in Daniel were so prophetically accurate that they have come under severe attack by secular skeptics over the past century with respect to their actual dating. There is much reason, as developed in detail by Grant Jeffrey and other theologians, to consider these attacks to be void of any merit whatsoever.

Example 15 - Luke 1:26-38:

"And in the sixth month the angel Gabriel was sent from God unto a city of Galilee, named Nazareth, To a virgin espoused to a man whose name was Joseph, of the house of David; and the virgin's name was Mary. And the angel came in unto her, and said, Hail, thou that art highly favored, the Lord is with thee: blessed art thou among women.

"And when she saw him, she was troubled at his saying, and cast in her mind what manner of salutation this should be.

"And the angel said unto her, Fear not, Mary: for thou hast found favor with God. And, behold, thou shalt conceive in thy womb, and bring forth a son, and shalt call his name Jesus. He shall be great, and shall be called the Son of the Highest; and the Lord God shall give unto him the throne of his father David: And he shall reign over the house of Jacob for ever; and of his kingdom there shall be no end.

"Then said Mary unto the angel, How shall this be, seeing I know not a man?

"And the angel answered and said unto her, The Holy Ghost shall come upon thee, and the power of the Highest shall overshadow thee; therefore also that holy thing which shall be born of thee shall be called the Son of God. And, behold, thy cousin Elisabeth, she hath also conceived a son in her old age; and this is the sixth month with her, who was called barren. For with God nothing shall be impossible.

"And Mary said, Behold the handmaid of the Lord; be it unto me according to thy word. And the angel departed from her."

It would be interesting to know what these angels actually looked like to Daniel and Mary. What is certain is that they both perceived these apparitions to be other than merely human.

Example 16 – Luke 24:1-7:

"Now upon the first day of the week, very early in the morning, they came unto the sepulcher, bringing the spices which they had prepared, and certain others with them. And they found the stone rolled away from the sepulcher. And they entered in, and found not the body of the Lord Jesus. And it came to pass, as they were much perplexed about this, behold, two men stood by them, in shining garments; and as they were afraid, and bowed down their faces to the earth, they said unto them, Why seek ye the living among the dead? He is not here, but is risen! Remember how he spoke unto you when He was yet in Galilee, Saying, The Son of man must be delivered into the hands of sinful men, and be crucified, and the third day rise again."

Example 17 - Luke 24:13-32:

"And, behold, two of them went that same day to a village called Emmaus, which was from Jerusalem about threescore furlongs. And they talked together of all these things which had happened. And it came to pass that, while they communed together and reasoned, Jesus Himself drew near, and went with them. But their eyes were holden that they should not recognize him. And He said unto them, What manner of communications are these that ye have one with another, as ye walk, and are sad? And the one of them, whose name was Cleopas, answering, said unto Him, Art thou only a stranger in Jerusalem, and hast no known the things which are come to pass there in these days? And He said unto them, What things? And they said unto Him, Concerning Jesus of Nazareth, who was a prophet, mighty in deed and word before God and all the people; and how the chief priests and our rulers delivered Him to be condemned to death, and have crucified Him. But we hoped that it had been He who should have redeemed Israel; and, besides all this, today is the third day since these things were done. Yea, and certain women also of our company amazed us, who were early at the sepulcher; and wen they found not His body, they came, saying that they had also seen a vision of angels, who said that He was alive.

"And certain of those who were with us went to the sepulcher, and found it even as the women had said; but Him they saw not. Then he said unto them, O foolishe ones, and slow of heart to believe all that the prophets have spoken! Ought not Christ to have suffered these things, and to enter into His glory? And beginning at Moses

and all the prophets, He expounded unto them, in all the Scriptures, the things concerning Himself.

"And they drew near unto the village, to which they went; and He made as though He would have gone farther. But they constrained Him, saying Abide with us; for it is toward evening, and the day is far spent. And He went in to tarry with them. And it came to pass, as He sat eating with them, He took bread, and blessed it, and broke it, and gave it to them. And their eyes were opened, and they recognized Him; and He vanished out of their sight. And they said one to another, Did not our heart burn within us, while He talked with us along the way, and while He opened to us the Scriptures?"

Example 18 – John 20:24-29:

"But Thomas, one of the twelve, called Didymus, was not with them when Jesus came. The other disciples, therefore, said unto him, We have seen the Lord. But he said unto them, Except I shall see in his hands the print of the nails, and put my finger into the print of the nails, and thrust my hand into his side, I will not believe. And, after eight days, again hi disciples were inside, and Thomas with them; then came Jesus, the doors being shut, and stood in the midst, and said, Peace be unto you.

"Then said He to Thomas, Reach here thy finger, and behold my hands; and reach here thy hand, and thrust it into my side; and be not faithless, but believing. And Thomas answered, and said unto Him, My Lord and my God.

"Jesus saith unto him, Thomas, because thou hast seen me, thou hast believed; blessed are they that have not seen, and yet have believed.

Example 19 – John 21:4-14:

"But when the morning was now come, Jesus stood on the shore; but the disciples knew not that it was Jesus. Then Jesus saith unto them, Children, have ye any food? They answered Him, No. And He said unto them, Cast the net on the right side of the boat and ye shall find. They cast, therefore, and now they were not able to draw it for the multitude of fish. Therefore, the disciple whom Jesus loved saith unto Peter, It is the Lord. Now when Simon Peter heard that it

was the lord, he girt his fisher' coat unto him (for he was naked), and did cast himself into the sea. And the other disciples came in a little boat (for they were not far from land, but as it were two hundred cubits), dragging the net with fish. As soon, then, as they were come to land, they saw a fire of coals there, and fish laid on it, and bread. Jesus saith unto them, Bring of the fish which ye have now caught. Simon Peter went up, and drew the net to land full of great fish, an hundred and fifty and three; and although there were so many, yet was not the net broken.

"Jesus saith unto them, Come and dine. And none of the disciples dared ask Him, who art thou? Knowing that it was the Lord. Jesus then cometh, and taketh bread, and giveth them, and fish likewise. This is now the third time that Jesus showed Himself to his disciples, after he was risen from the dead."

Example 20 - Acts 8:1-4, 9:1-1-9

"And Saul was consenting unto [Stephen's] death. And at that time there was a great persecution against the church which was at Jerusalem; and they were all scattered abroad throughout the regions of Judah and Samaria, except the apostles. And devout men carried Stephen to his burial, and made great lamentation over him. As for Saul, he made havoc of the church, entering into every house, and haling men and women committed them to prison. Therefore they that were scattered abroad went every where preaching the word."

"And Saul, yet breathing out threatenings and slaughter against the disciples of the Lord, went unto the high priest, And desired of him letters to Damascus to the synagogues, that if he found any of this way, whether they were men or women, he might bring them bound unto Jerusalem.

"And as he journeyed, he came near Damascus: and suddenly there shined round about him a light from heaven: And he fell to the earth, and heard a voice saying unto him, Saul, Saul, why persecutest thou me?

"And he said, Who art thou, Lord? And the Lord said, I am Jesus whom thou persecutest: it is hard for thee to kick against the pricks.

"And he trembling and astonished said, Lord, what wilt thou have me to do? And the Lord said unto him, Arise, and go into the city, and it shall be told thee what thou must do.

"And the men which journeyed with him stood speechless, hearing a voice, but seeing no man. And Saul arose from the earth; and when his eyes were opened, he saw no man: but they led him by the hand, and brought him into Damascus. And he was three days without sight, and neither did eat nor drink."

The following excerpts from the Bible, which are merely 'tips of the iceberg', demonstrate how thoroughly this encounter turned Paul's life around.

Example 21 - Acts 9:10-20, Romans 1:1-8:

"And there was a certain disciple at Damascus, named Ananias; and to him said the Lord in a vision, Ananias. And he said, Behold, I am here, Lord.

"And the Lord said unto him, Arise, and go into the street which is called Straight, and inquire in the house of Judas for one called Saul, of Tarsus: for, behold, he prayeth, And hath seen in a vision a man named Ananias coming in, and putting his hand on him, that he might receive his sight.

"Then Ananias answered, Lord, I have heard by many of this man, how much evil he hath done to thy saints at Jerusalem: And here he hath authority from the chief priests to bind all that call on thy name.

"But the Lord said unto him, Go thy way: for he is a chosen vessel unto me, to bear my name before the Gentiles, and kings, and the children of Israel; For I will show him how great things he must suffer for my name's sake."

"Paul [Saul], a servant of Jesus Christ, called to be an apostle, separated unto the gospel of God, (Which he had promised afore by his prophets in the holy Scriptures,) Concerning his Son Jesus Christ our Lord, which was made of the seed of David according to the flesh; And declared to be the Son of God with power, according to the Spirit of holiness, by the resurrection from the dead: By whom we have received grace and apostleship, for obedience to the faith

among all nations, for his name: Among whom are ye also the called of Jesus Christ: To all that be in Rome, beloved of God, called to be saints: Grace to you and peace, from God our Father and the Lord Jesus Christ.

"First, I thank my God through Jesus Christ for you all, that your faith is spoken of throughout the whole world."

Here again we see evidence that the encounter imparted wisdom; it totally and permanently changed Saul's mentality and his life. Note particularly the intimacy of Paul's appreciation of Jesus Christ as opposed to his previous anger-filled rejection of Him.

Example 22 – Hebrews 13:2:

"Be not forgetful to entertain strangers; for thereby some have entertained angels unawares."

Example 23 - Revelation 1:9-20:

"I John, who also am your brother, and companion in tribulation, and in the kingdom and patience of Jesus Christ, was in the isle that is called Patmos, for the word of God, and for the testimony of Jesus Christ.

"I was in the Spirit on the Lord's day, and heard behind me a great voice, as of a trumpet, Saying, I am Alpha and Omega, the first and the last: and, What thou seest, write in a book, and send it unto the seven churches which are in Asia; unto Ephesus, and unto Smyrna, and unto Pergamos, and unto Thyatira, and unto Sardis, and unto Philadelphia, and unto Laodicea.

"And I turned to see the voice that spake with me. And being turned, I saw seven golden candlesticks; And in the midst of the seven candlesticks one like unto the Son of man, clothed with a garment down to the foot, and girt about the paps with a golden girdle. His head and his hairs were white as snow; and his eyes were as a flame of fire; And his feet like unto fine brass, as if they burned in a furnace; and his voice as the sound of many waters. And he had in his right hand seven stars: and out of his mouth went a sharp two-edged sword: and his countenance was as the sun shineth in his strength.

"And when I saw him, I fell at his feed as dead. And he laid his right hand upon me, saying unto me, Fear not; I am the first and the last: I am he that liveth, and was dead; and, behold, I am alive for evermore, Amen; and have the keys of hell and death.

"Write the things which thou hast seen, and the things which are, and the things which shall be hereafter; The mystery of the seven stars which thou sawest in my right hand, and the seven golden candlesticks. The seven stars are the angels of the seven churches: and the seven candlesticks which thou sawest are the seven churches."

This close encounter with the risen Jesus follows a pattern that is seen throughout the Bible, that of an apparition who imparts wisdom and understanding that reaches out beyond our human abilities and our conception of time. In every case, the knowledge and information dovetails perfectly with other parts of the Bible, contributing to a consistent whole.

The involvement of past UFOs in Scripture should not be surprising, particularly to Christians. If it is, we must acknowledge the fact that we have been taught and conditioned by a secular society and its institutions that wish to deny the existence of God at every turn in favor of a rigid materialism. The materialistic mindset, with its insistence that in the unlikely event that UFOs actually exist they would be materialistic devices from another material planet like our own, has led to nothing but confusion and dead-end speculations regarding UFOs.

Given our faith in the God of Judeo-Christian tradition, we must necessarily assume that if UFOs exist, God is involved. As Creator of the universe He created all that exists within it, including the things we call UFOs regardless of whether they exist within or outside our imaginations. It matters very little whether these objects are primarily physical or spiritual, for even the casual reader of the Bible knows that God's domain includes both. In that sense, our own technological wonders, our Mars rovers and space shuttles, including their operators, belong to God. This is anything but a trivial issue. The notion of UFOs as technology-adept aliens comes straight out of the more far-reaching purely secular notion that God as an Entity who is personally involved in and relevant to our lives does not exist. The fact that most of us fail to appreciate is that our understanding of the ultimate ownership of our universe is perhaps the most influential element of how we have perceived UFO events in the past, and of whether we consider them to be basically good or evil.

Regardless of their origin, however, their current reputation is not so good, and at least part of the blame can be placed on their behavior toward us. Based on their perceived secrecy, apparent indifference toward humans, and the terror which they evoke in those whom they abduct, it would seem reasonable to suggest that they come from the wrong side of the good-bad line. Perhaps some of them do. But as one reviews the many abduction accounts and their supposed horrors, one gets the unmistakable impression that the most terrifying aspect of these encounters is the lack of control experienced by the abductees: being under the absolute dominance of their captor conflicts sharply with their materialistic, probably godless view of life and their place in it. Accustomed to perceiving themselves as self-driven, they are forced to confront an absolute powerlessness to escape the situation or to influence the unfolding of the event. In *Witnessed*, Budd Hopkins captures the essence of this aspect:

"When UFO abductees come upon evidence that, for them, confirms the physical reality of their encounters, their reactions are invariably shock and depression. No one I have ever worked with has indicated pleasure or relief at any kind of confirming news. Treating their UFO memories as earthly, explainable dreams or fantasies is for abductees a necessary hope, a bulwark of denial against the unthinkable. But when that protective dam bursts and the abductees' tightly held systems of defense are swept away, they are left with a frightening and intolerable truth."

For many 'victims', the experience flies in the face of the way they were taught to believe regarding the ultimate independence of the individual, their understanding of themselves as being masters of their own destinies. Most of us, whether our backgrounds were religious or not, tend to compartmentalize our religious meditations, separating them from the everyday reality of our lives. When we think of God, we perceive our thoughts to be of our own volition, another exercise of free will. We rarely perceive our relation with God in terms of His absolute dominance over our lives. For the most part, God appears to be content with this arrangement.

But there are significant exceptions. A review of the encounters experienced by Daniel, Paul, and John, for example, demonstrates quite clearly that they were welcomed as life-altering events, but sometimes well after the fact. The experiences had many of the same characteristics of modern UFO abductions. They involved discomfort and terror as well, even for these individuals who had an unusually intimate relationship with God.

I would suggest that if the modern abduction experience is perceived as a negative one, it is because the absolute dominance of the 'occupants' over their subjects conflicts so greatly with the secular world view held by most of us. Should we blame the UFOs for this, or should we instead understand how far from God we have put ourselves?

CHAPTER TWENTY SIX

Alien or Not?

Does the historical evidence of 'aliens' collected by secular scholars actually indicate something other than alien? It appears that even secular accounts of enigmatic events reaching back in time hint of associations with our Judeo-Christian God.

Among the most spectacular of extraterrestrial accounts from the past is the collection of the religious beliefs of the Dogon tribe in Mali, West Africa. It is an astonishing story of information this tribe possesses that should never have been available to them in their isolation and primitive state of existence. As related by Scott Alan Roberts in Chapter 5 of his book *The Rise and Fall of the Nephilim,* French anthropologists Marcel Griaule and Germaine Dieterlen extracted from their religious mythology a wealth of information regarding the star Sirius and its associated system the accuracy of which is simply beyond the tribe's powers of observation, or indeed beyond the observational capability of any earthbound society. A brief summary of Roberts' account of their incredible customs and the information they represent is given below.

The Dogon people have a tradition, reaching into the unknown past, of worshiping beings they call the Nommos. These froglike creatures aren't local to the area, but reside somewhat farther away, within hailing distance of the star Sirius B. They recognize Sirius B as one member of a dual-star system, and depict in their drawings the two stars, Sirius A and Sirius B as rotating about each other in an elliptical pattern. Western society figured out elliptical orbits only after the pioneering work of German astronomer Johannes Kepler in the seventeenth century. The Dogons probably beat him to the concept as there was no known modern interaction between the Dogons and the Western world until the 1920s.

The Dogon legend describes the Nommos as having lived on a planet that orbits Sirius B. They arrived on Earth in a craft that we would describe as an ark, which descended in a spin and landed with a big commotion.

The Nommo furnished information to the Dogons; eventually, one of them was crucified on a tree, was resurrected, and returned to the Sirius star system.

A more detailed view of the Dogons and their strange religion is presented by Robert Temple in his 1998 book *The Sirius Mystery*.

As explained by Temple, there's a mystery indeed about the Dogon knowledge of the Sirius star system. Sirius A is visible, but Sirius B is much smaller, being a dwarf star, and is invisible to the observer on earth, even with a decent telescope. Yet, as it is very dense, it possesses an appreciable gravitational field. The Dogons know that it is comparably tiny, because they named the star after the seed of an indigenous plant, the botanical name of which is digitaria. The seed of the digitaria is minute, being the smallest seed of which the Dogon are aware. Yet the Dogon consider the much larger star Sirius A to be unimportant to them next to the Nommo home star of Sirius B.

Moreover, the Dogons have the orbital period of Sirius B, which is fifty years, pegged with precision to its actual period, and understand that it rotates about its own axis, a common characteristic of stars.

The Dogons are also aware of planetary features within our own solar system. For example, they know that the moon is dead, that a ring encircles Saturn, and that Jupiter possesses four major moons. As for the Earth, it is understood to turn on its own axis and to make a great circle around the sun.

Temple's book includes other knowledge possessed by the Dogons. This additional information is simply too extensive for the scope of this book. Temple also apeculates, like Zecharia Sitchin who published *The Twelfth Planet* in 1976, that the evidence of the aliens' visitation is encoded in the traditions and literature of the ancient Mediterranean region, from which the Dogons, as well as the Greeks and Romans, borrowed from a common source.

Other societies, considered by us to be primitive, also worshiped beings that we like to label as "alien". Erich Von Daniken was the earliest of the modern investigators to popularize this practice. In his book *Chariots of the Gods?* Published in 1976, the same year that Sitchin published *The Twelfth Planet*, he cites many artifacts of unknown antiquity which don't fit into mainstream assumptions of man's history, noting that these oddities are either ignored by scientists or suffer the application of unsatisfactory reasons for their existence. Among these artifacts scattered about the world are structures of sophisticated design and immense proportions, the components of which are of equally impressive size. There are also, in widely scattered locations, structures, objects, and patterns on the ground with evident links to air or space travel.

The enigmatic straight lines in Nazca, Peru are ancient. Yet investigators can comprehend no useful purpose for them other than aircraft runways. There are also huge figures cut into the surface in the vicinity which are not recognizable on the ground, but are readily understood for what they are from an aerial perspective.

An abundance of enormous stone structures can be found high in the Andes Mountains of Peru and Bolivia and elsewhere in South and Central America. Von Daniken describes monolithic stone blocks weighing 10, 20, and 100 tons, with precisely defined edges, used in the construction of these structures. Some of the blocks are engraved with figures. Other figures are themselves carved out of stone. But the figures aren't quite human. Some have four fingers; others wear what appear to be helmets. Still others are depicted as flying.

In addition to artifacts which display a sophistication quite beyond what mainstream archaeologists are willing to attribute to the peoples of antiquity, there is an apparent knowledge itself that runs counter to our perception of ancient man and his lack of sophistication: maps, calendars and astronomical tables, texts, and even artifacts which demonstrate a knowledge of electricity and electro-chemical processes.

Maps of world scope found in the possession of eighteenth Century Turkish Admiral Piri Reis were not only amazingly accurate but depicted the Antarctic Continent as if it was ice-free, showing land boundaries and mountain ranges in their proper relative locations, although such boundaries were not known in modern times until the middle of the twentieth century. As Von Daniken pointed out, some of the maps appeared to researchers to represent data taken from aerial photographs. Believed to be of still greater antiquity than the sea captain to whom they belonged, the originals from which they were copied were probably created long before the time when the world thought that the earth was flat.

A calendar of impressive sophistication was found in Tiahuanaco. This device gave the equinoxes, seasons, and hourly positions of the moon. Halfway around the world, archaeologists digging at the Mesopotamian site of Nineveh found a mathematical calculation carried out to 15 digits, when, as Von Daniken pointed out, mathematicians of the much-later Greek civilization couldn't count above 10,000.

Artifacts found in the Middle East and China whose fabrication required a knowledge of electricity and electrochemistry include batteries and battery electrodes, crystal lenses which we can make only with the electrochemically-produced cesium oxide, and objects fashioned of platinum and aluminum.

Where did this enigmatic ancient knowledge come from? Von Daniken asserts that it came from visitors to Earth from space. He speculates briefly at one point that these visitors may have come from the planet Mars before its surface was destroyed by some cosmic event. Elsewhere he places their origin farther afield, among one of the star systems in our Milky Way Galaxy. He claims that we can see depictions of these beings in ancient artwork, from cave drawings scattered throughout the world to Sumerian cylinder seals and South American stone carvings.

But above all the mute artifacts we find scattered about the earth, we have the ancient literature that brings these visitors to life. All we have to do, Von Daniken asserts, is to discard the mundane, inaccurate interpretation of these tales that was first initiated by scholars of the eighteenth and nineteenth centuries, a time when the technology to which they pointed was simply inconceivable. Less than two centuries ago, the notion of traveling about the Earth in flying vehicles was considered an absurdity by all but a few visionaries. The thought of traveling among the planets in space vehicles was at the far end of science fiction well into the last century.

Now that we ourselves possess much of the technology described in the ancient literature, however, we can see these texts as representing potential truth rather than necessarily depicting flights of fancy. In line with a more technically-oriented interpretation of these ancient tales, flights of the 'gods' in aircraft and space vehicles appears to have been a common theme.

Von Daniken notes that the Bible itself is a part of that ancient literature which describes flying machines driven by 'gods'. He refers to the multi-winged, multi-wheeled flying vehicle described by the prophet Ezekiel as what modern man would call a 'UFO'. The prophet Elijah may have ascended to heaven in a similar vehicle. Whatever these vehicles were, they certainly represented a technology far in advance of what we consider the peoples of that day to have possessed. The only other alternative to the physical reality of those vehicles described in the Bible is that they were dreams or visions of Ezekiel and others. But if that is the case, from whence did these highly-detailed visions come? It is absurd to think that they were simply figments of active imaginations. To deny that the vehicles actually existed is equivalent to asserting that the visions came from God. Consequently, in either case there is some truth to their existence.

While *Chariots of the Gods?*, first published in 1970, was a best-seller, Von Daniken was considered by many at the time to be a sensationalist. Respected theologians remained indifferent to his views, treating the notion of space aliens as a mere passing fad, to be indulged in by those whose literary tastes run to those expressed by the supermarket tabloids. Much of Von Daniken's work, however, is insightful enough to merit more respect than he has received from the mainstream religious community. Since Von Daniken, moreover, others have taken up this particular baton with quite serious scholarship. Notable among these researchers is Zecharia Sitchin, who authored the *Earth Chronicles* book series centered on his *12th Planet* concept.

Many aspects of Sitchin's arguments are not original with him. He repeats a variety of facts and conclusions that were presented before by Von Daniken. Nevertheless, like many scholars who flesh out the pioneering work of others in greater detail, Sitchin brings out a wealth of additional background information in support of Von Daniken's original claims. Furthermore, his theories regarding the source of the cosmic visitors do indeed appear to involve some original concepts which add depth to the discussion. Because of his scholarship, consistency of thought, and clarity of presentation, Sitchin's writings will be included with Von Daniken's as the generally representative focus of discussion.

Regardless of whether one agrees with part or all of Sitchin's thesis, he presents a good case, providing in the process a very concise, readable story of how the history of man developed through the eyes of nineteenth and twentieth century archaeologists. As Sitchin follows the successive discoveries of the sites of ancient near-Eastern civilizations, he manages to convey a sense of excitement over the archaeologists' growing grasp of the information which was revealed therein and of his own developing realization of the enormous implications of their discoveries. The civilization of man, Sitchin asserts in *The 12th Planet*, began in the fourth millenium B.C. along the Euphrates River just above the Persian Gulf, at Eridu in the Biblical land of Shinar which modern historians call Sumer. Its expansion from there followed the Tigris and Euphrates Rivers into Akkadia and Babylon, and from thence northward into the region of Mount Ararat and eventually into Europe, westward via the Mediterranean Sea to Crete and then Greece, back southward along the eastern bank of the Mediterranean into Canaan and Egypt, and eastward into the Indus Valley. Its northward progression was facilitated by the Horites (Hurrians), who communicated with the Akkadian civilization to their south and the Hittites to their north.

The change that the civilization of Sumer represented from the primitive lifestyle of man up to that time was so sudden that scholars called it astonishing. Modern society could easily identify with it: it had a Government with a bicameral congress, a code of laws including those to protect the poor (preceding Hammurabi by almost a millenium), schools, artistic sophistication, music with the flavor of our own Country/Western music, a pantheistic religion of twelve primary dieties which formed the basis of the Grecian, Roman, Canaanite, Hittite, Amorite, and Egyptian systems of worship, and a written language which was passed on to these same societies. Its people practiced law, medicine, agriculture, studied mathematics and history, and concerned themselves with world peace. These very facts are what initially motivated and continue to support the assertions that I made in *Marching to a Worthy Drummer* regarding our common basic misunderstanding of our own history.

Sitchin claims that the rise of the Sumerian civilization was too abrupt to have been accomplished by man alone. The suddenness of man's progress there led Sitchin to surmise that man was given a big push by outside influences. Mankind had help, he says, and that help came from beyond earth. Moreover, he claims, the Bible speaks of it. In his book *The 12th Planet,* Sitchin interprets the Biblical book of Genesis as describing humanoid beings from another planet who visited earth many thousands of years ago. Their first and principal occupation was in the region of ancient Sumer, where they built several cities. The Sumerian name for the region was E.din, which means 'home of the righteous ones'. The Biblical implication of this name is obvious.

Portions of the Bible, as a matter of fact, have a startling similarity to some recently-decipered Sumerian texts. To support his view that humans were visited by aliens, Sitchin points out the many Sumerian, Biblical, and other ancient records alluding to 'gods' who possessed an advanced technology having characteristics paralleling those of our modern age, including flight above the earth and into space. He also shows that mankind, while venerating these beings as gods, attributed curiously human characteristics to them, chief of which was their ability to mate and have offspring. They also had shortcomings of a human nature, such as jealousies, anger, untruthfulness, unfaithfulness, and self-serving motives. These records, Sitchin asserts, are consistent with passages in the Bible, if those passages are interpreted from the perspective of an alien presence on earth which, despite its advanced technology, fell far short of the Godhood which mankind attributed to it.

Among this ancient literature is a rich and colorful tradition of dieties who form a family dynasty. The members of this dynasty are subject to the same nobility and moral faults as mankind. Stories of their personalities, the relationships among themselves and with mankind, and their exploits form a cosmic drama whose main players seem to be somewhat akin to the characters of the old television series *Dallas*. Indeed, their loves, jealousies, sexual liaisons, and adventures would make good material for a television soap opera.

Sitchin notes a close correlation between the pantheon of gods in other cultures and their Sumerian counterparts. He furnishes compelling evidence to support his claim that this Sumerian pantheon was the basis of the Hittite, Egyptian, Greek, and Roman religious systems, and that Sumerian knowledge and religious concepts greatly influenced religious thought throughout the world, including that of the Hindus and the Hebrews. The Egyptians, for example, believed that their gods came from a far land, most likely in the region of ancient Sumer, after the Deluge. In fact, the primary deities associated with both earthly and heavenly activities and celestial bodies, in particular, have been accepted among many archaelogists as having originated in Sumer. Sitchin notes, in support of this supposition, that the hierarchical structure of the gods, which was maintained at a constant number of 12 in the Sumerian pantheon as some of them were replaced by others, was similarly maintained at 12 in the later Egyptian, Greek, and Roman pantheons.

There is some minor overlap of material between Sitchin and Temple, but it is not known to what extent they may have shared data, if at all. There are, however, significant differences in focus. Where Sitchin primarily (but not exclusively) references Mesopotamian, i.e. Sumerian and later Akkadian and Babylonian, clues to extraterrestrial visitations, Temple extracts his information from historically more recent source data, including epics and myths from Egypt, Greece, Rome and other civilizations from the Mediterranean area. Temple engages in much speculation out of a comparative review of mythology and word roots. His primary intellectual tools are an unusually comprehensive knowledge base of legends and myths, an impressive memory, and a rather freely-employed flair for creative associations. Many of his associations are tenuous at best, while others are somewhat more plausible. Although his treatment often lacks the integrating theses which other authors such as Sitchin employ to tie together the various components of their developments, the sheer aggregation of the associations gives weight even to some of his more tenuous connections. Temple believes, as Sitchin does, that an extensive knowledge was imparted to mankind 5,000 or so years ago. A part of this knowledge, elements of which it is highly unlikely that man could have obtained on his own, concerned the Sirius star system, as noted in the commentary above regarding the Dogon tribe of Mali, Africa.

Temple went on to claim that the knowledge which the Dogons possess is but the tip of the iceberg: the Greeks as well as the Dogons borrowed this knowledge from the more ancient Sumerian and Egyptian civilizations, which were not only contemporary with but in communication with each other. Intrinsic to their common knowledge were the same elements which the Dogon most probably borrowed and display in their rituals: understanding of the Sirius system, including the small size and great density of Sirius B, its approximately 50-year orbit about Sirius A, and the ellipticity of the orbit. Greek language and mythology, he asserts, encodes a somewhat imperfectly-understood vestige of this ancient knowledge and its associated rituals.

Temple, like Von Daniken, supports his thesis of alien visitations with the observation of records of strange hybrid partly-human, partly-animal creatures. According to Temple, the creatures, some of which were considered to be quite ugly and fear-inspiring, were supposedly intelligent, extremely knowledgeable, and adept in the arts of civilization. He implies that the aliens themselves may have had these forms. Von Daniken, on the other hand, attributes these forms to experimentation on species indigenous to the Earth. A variety of such beings, mostly amphibious but sometimes possessing features of snakes or other creatures instead of fins in their lower parts, were depicted in the ancient art of a number of societies, including the Dogon, Chinese, and especially the Egyptians. It is only with recent advances in genetic science that we can perceive the possibility that the depictions represent reality: perhaps at some time in the distant past there was much experimentation with gene splicing or tampering with epigenetic elements. In *Gods from Outer Space*, Von Daniken notes the many references to hybrid creatures in ancient literature and art from the Sumerian civilization forward. As he implied in *The Eyes of the Sphinx*, the many odd forms of artifacts uncovered in Egypt, which often combine portions of vastly different species, indicate that the genetic manipulation may have attempted to cross species boundaries. Whatever the origin of these odd creatures, the depictions appear to represent something other than fiction. They lend weight to the alien thesis.

But in reviewing the works of these authors of the historical alien genre, one can discern a number of common assumptions that are not necessarily true, and, in fact, severely restrict their visions of our past. Their primary assumption is that the Bible, while it might contain interesting and perhaps even valuable historic information, is just another document written by men. As such, there is nothing in it that can be attributed to the influence of God, nor is the majority of information treated by it as fact anything more than oft-repeated fable. Even the fables are considered to be degenerations of earlier, more accurate accounts. Several other assumptions directly follow this first one, especially the notion of evolution – that mankind, in opposition to the events catalogued in Genesis, evolved from a lesser creature, and from a primitive state to increasing levels of sophistication. In lockstep with the theory of evolution and equally opposed to the notion of Biblical truth is the companion doctrine of uniformitarianism, that the present is the key to the past and the state of the earth and life within it as we see it today is the result of billions of years of slowly-working processes. With the rejection of Scripture as truth, God Himself doesn't seem to be particularly relevant to science, or even history for that matter. Thus in attempting to address the UFO phenomenon, God isn't seen as particularly relevant to that issue either, and the researchers are left to their pursuit of answers along the lines of cutting-edge technology. When researchers find evidence of technical sophistication in our historical past, the rigid constraints that they impose on themselves by their godlessness impels them toward one of only two possible answers: either mankind was visited in the past by technologically superior beings, or there is insufficient data to say what went on in the ancient past and the subject would be best left alone (for now). This is why the group of investigators who are interested in ancient technology are predominantly spokespersons for UFO visitations in the past.

What if the Bible is historically accurate after all? Then it's immediately another ball game. According to Genesis 6:1-7, we started out with a lot of talent, and quickly became corrupted, probably worshiping the same inventive spirit within ourselves that modern man does:

> "And it came to pass, when men began to multiply on the face of the earth, and daughters were born unto them, That the sons of God saw the daughters of men that they were fair; and they took them wives of all which they chose. And the Lord said, My Spirit shall not always strive with man, for that he also is flesh: yet his days shall be a hundred and twenty years.

> "There were giants in the earth in those days; and also after that, when the sons of God came in unto the daughters of men, and they bare children to them, the same became mighty men which were of old, men of renown.

> "And God saw that the wickedness of man was great in the earth, and that every imagination of the thoughts of his heart was only evil continually. And it repented the Lord that he had made man on

the earth, and it grieved him at his heart. And the Lord said, I will destroy man whom I have created from the face of the earth; both man, and beast, and the creeping thing, and the fowls of the air; for it repenteth me that I have made them."

With God in the picture, we would no longer need ancient aliens to account for the Nazca Lines, the Great Pyramid, the Egyptian Tombs, and a host of other intriguing archaeological relics. Intelligent and sophisticated humans may have existed in the ancient past, turning into cave-dwelling primitives only temporarily until they recovered from the necessity for mere survival following the Great Flood. Perhaps their technology even surpassed our own. After all, it took us less than 400 years after we got on the technology wagon to achieve the sophistication in the mathematical and physical sciences that led to automotive transportation, manned flight, supersonic flight, space flight, worldwide communication, radio, television, computers, robotics, bridges, tunnels, skyscrapers and gameboys.

Actually, it is no longer logical to reject the historical accuracy of the Bible in favor of the opposing pseudoscience. Not after the the notion of uniformitarianism, at best a conceptual tool but not a very good one at that, has pretty much received a well-deserved comeuppance, with numerous former adherents rushing to discard it. With the arrival on the scientific scene of fresh new insights into the process of life, especially at the submicroscopic level, the theory of evolution is following suit, only not so quickly. The major hindrance to its utter rejection is the lack of any other theory of life's origins that doesn't involve God.

PART EIGHT

THE ANGELIC
CONNECTION

CHAPTER TWENTY SEVEN

UFO Encounters and the Near-Death Experience

Dr. Hynek's ultimate inclusion of spiritual involvement into the UFO issue opened the door very slightly to the consideration of the phenomena as being something other than purely secular. A few interested people began to wonder: could UFOs actually have something to do with God's domain? Those who saw a connection between modern UFO events and similar accounts in the Bible saw in these earlier stories much angelic activity. In Genesis alone, in chapters 6, 18, and 28, as detailed in a previous chapter, the beings interacting with men were specifically identified as angels.

But most people of Hynek's era declined to think of that possibility. The basic reality of UFOs was still very questionable. The issue of actual existence continued to dominate the public mind to the extent of limiting the topic to that of passing interest. Through the years of our modern exposure to this phenomenon, public acceptance has often been enthusiastic but fleeting, being strongly influenced by media bias. Interest has waxed and waned periodically just like the UFO flaps which books of that era describe. But even during the quiet times the public never entirely forgot the fact that something did happen in the skies, and that the usual commonplace explanations just didn't account for what took place. By the turn of the century polls discovered that a significant percentage of the public believed in the existence of UFOs. The belief itself, however, has been weak and fuzzy until recently for two primary reasons: first, because it didn't fit well with the naturalistic system of thought by which our secular institutions wished us to perceive the world about us; and second, because the notion itself had been trivialized, falsely- and under-reported, and otherwise discouraged by what we consider to be 'official' sources of information. Given that disconnect, we had tended to compartmentalize whatever knowledge we might have possessed regarding the phenomenon away from our bases of everyday reality. Reality existed over here. The UFO issue was over there. With few exceptions, even those who have had first-hand experience with the objects or their occupants had in the past performed this mental process of separation.

The barriers which historically have served to impose this separation not only remain in place, but are more firmly entrenched than ever. The issue is not with the UFO phenomenon itself. Despite the media trivialization and official denials, interactions between people and UFOs continue unabated, often involving mass sightings which are difficult to deny.

The real separation issue resides in the power of the media over the public mind, supported by the increasing regression of our ability to think and act for ourselves. We the public have come to expect the media to do the thinking for us, and the media have been all too happy to oblige, to the extent that social engineering is now an integral part of the media agenda. One of our favorite television shows is *Blue Bloods*. Nevertheless, Carolyn and I frequently encounter situational scenes in the series that cause us to turn to each other and mouth in unison "social engineering". It's hard any more to come across shows that don't so indulge in supporting the latest political correctness buzz.

Unfortunately, the media mentality is dominated by the thoroughly secular paradigm of naturalism. In practice, if the UFO phenomenon is under-reported by the media, any linkage therein between UFOs and angelic activity is essentially nonexistent.

At infrequent intervals the public is treated to a particularly spectacular or undeniable sighting event, but the coverage rarely continues beyond a day. With no subsequent media follow-up, the event rather rapidly departs from the public awareness, with much of the public assessment of it being consigned to the hoax category despite the existing cynical attitude of the general public toward both the media and government spokespersons. If the media do not constantly remind us of them, UFOs gravitate quickly back to the dusty, lonely and rarely-visited recesses of the public mind. Nowhere does the media offer the slightest support to the possibility that UFOs might have something to do with God, with the sole exception of the Catholic press coverage of apparitions of 'Mary'. Nor will they ever do so, barring some extraordinary event.

The situation with the reporting of near-death experiences (NDEs) is even worse. There, the connection with God being obvious, the absence of media coverage is even more conspicuous.

Actually, there are at least seven important commonalities between UFO encounters and NDEs. The first of these, at least to those who see a religious connotation to the UFO encounter, is the angelic involvement in both. Second, both kinds of events include both positive and negative encounters. Third, many people, both those involved and their investigators, commonly interpret the experiences as negative. The account below involving the nun's NDE response may be distressingly typical. Fourth, the experiences are other-worldly; they don't fit into the pattern of what we consider to be normal. Fifth, the perceived capabilities of spiritual entities, including those involved in NDE experiences, extend beyond those of us who are confined to the material world. These super-powers include the ability to travel at will through the air without supporting devices, invisibility, and lack of solidity. Jesus' post-resurrection encounter with Thomas as described in John 20:24-29 and noted in a previous chapter, was of this flavor. Sixth, both types of experiences imparted knowledge that would be unobtainable through normal channels of information. The seventh is the most important of all: to those including myself who experienced positive encounters, there was a deep sense of loss at leaving behind the encounter environment.

These commonalities deserve to be addressed in greater detail. As for the angelic quality of the experiences, John Burke describes in his 2015 book *Imagine Heaven* multiple cases where the person involved was met by beings who were intuitively sensed to be angels. Of course, the "light at the end of the tunnel" that is included in so many of these events almost invariably has been associated with Jesus Christ. The same may be said regarding those UFO encounters that were experienced or interpreted as having religious components – the occupants of these craft were thought to be angelic in nature, whether the experience itself was positive or negative. In fact, both the NDE and UFO experiences included both positive and negative instances, where the negative NDE experience was often interpreted as being in hell, and the negative UFO event was attributed to demonic beings. As for the interpretation of an NDE experience as negative, John Burke relates one incident that may be more typical than we'd like to think. On page 41 of *Imagine Heaven* he quotes a woman who had her NDE experience in a Catholic hospital. After overcoming her fear of rejection over the matter, she shared her experience with a nurse. Just as she'd imagined, the nurse was horrified and sent for a nun to counsel her. The nun attributed the experience to the work of the devil. This reminds me of several Christian spokespersons who also attribute demonic inspiration to the UFO phenomenon. On the positive side, if the NDE subject went somewhere, that 'somewhere' was heaven, and for the 'religious' UFO encounter where knowledge was imparted, the subject in at least one case was instructed about or given visions of heaven. That particular case happened to be mine. Regarding the other-worldly nature of both types of experiences, this quality is evidenced by the large number of people who prefer to deny the reality of the events as delusional. It is common knowledge that UFO occupants and their craft perform maneuvers that are quite beyond the capabilities of mankind. Those involved in NDE experiences also claim to possess capabilities that go beyond the normal range of human experience. It's not always appreciated that Jesus Himself demonstrated super-normal capabilities in addition to His healings, both before and after His resurrection. John 8:59 illustrates this quality of Jesus. In that passage, when they were about to stone Him, He made Himself unrecognizable to them and went out from the temple "in the midst" of those surrounding Him who wished to do Him harm.

Regarding the impartation of knowledge, I detailed in Part One my own experience, which not only gave me the desire to acquire knowledge of Scripture but the actual understanding that was given to me that can't be explained in any other way. I expand on that single incident by noting the prophetic knowledge that was given to a number of Biblical figures. Some of it is spectacular, including Daniel's forecast in Daniel 9:24-27 of the timing of critical events that would occur in the future, including Jesus' entrance as King into Jerusalem a certain time from a predicted event. This prophecy was fulfilled to the exact day hundreds of years in the future from Daniel's life! Another prophetic event that was precisely fulfilled was Ezekiel's forecast of Israel's return to statehood in 1948, as demonstrated by the late Bible scholar Grant Jeffrey and as I describe in my novel *Cathy* and touch upon in Appendix Four to *Marching to a Worthy Drummer*."

Some very impressive knowledge, beyond what humans are capable of acquiring, comes out of NDE experiences as well. On pages 35 and 36 of *Imagine Heaven*, Burke relates how people who have been blind from birth emerge from their NDE episodes with descriptions of persons and objects that would be accessible only to those with the ability to see. He presents a particularly poignant example on page 48 of how a Dutch couple had a daughter they named Reitje who had died while a child. Eventually, after a period of grieving, they had a son. They refrained from telling him about their daughter, wishing to wait until he was older and could better handle the topic of death. When he was five, the son contracted meningitis and died. When he was resuscitated, his greatly-relieved parents came to his hospital bedside to shower him with their love, whereupon he told them that he had gone to heaven. He told them that he had met his sister there, and gave them her name of Reitje. He asked them why they had never told him about her, saying that she had hugged him and was very loving toward them all. It blows my mind to think how the boy's parents must have reacted to that news.

A lovely lady with whom I had worked at one time confided in me her own near-death experience. While giving birth to her last baby, she succumbed to uncontrollable bleeding, and died on the hospital bed. She recalled hovering under the ceiling above her body, where they were working to resuscitate her. One of the doctors was talking to the nurse assisting him, and happened to make some inappropriate remarks about her. When she regained consciousness, she called him to her bedside and, as the astonished man began to melt down, redressed him sharply for what he had said.

I seem to have acquired some knowledge about heaven. In my most recent novel *Home, Sweet Heaven* I continue with the adventures of Earl and Joyce Cook, some of which involve the spiritual realm of heaven. An excerpt of their first encounter with that realm is given below; I was comfortable with the writing, as if I was happily recalling it directly from memory.

"They entered the light and emerged into a scene of awesome splendor. It was familiar, even homey, as if she'd been here before, long before her journey on earth. She was surrounded by greenery more vivid and lush than what she'd been used to on earth. . . . Beyond the grandness of the visual experience, love was in the very air, so immense that it seemed to have a palpable presence. Her sense of familiarity strengthened as, mingled with the love was the growing knowledge that this was her real home.

"Yes!" a laughing angel affirmed to her without speaking. The presence of this being, Joyce realized with shock, was not outside her own soul. The being was within her, part of her own self and anything but an invasion of her privacy. Privacy here was meaningless, her spiritual intuition told her, as unwelcome as such an intrusion would have represented in the material world from which she had so recently departed. The intimacy was akin to romance with perhaps even an implication of sensuality in its connectivity, but extended vastly beyond the earthly experience. Another spiritual being entered their domain, extending the joy of intimate communion.

"'Oh!' Joyce exclaimed to her new companion. 'Oh my, I recognize you! You're Cathy!' The recognition of the soul who in earth had inhabited the severely crippled body of a girl afflicted with cerebral palsy overwhelmed her and she began to cry. Cathy joined in, weeping with joy and tightening their spiritual bond. 'Look at me!' she cried, moving outside Joyce's domain momentarily to prance. 'I'm whole!' She skipped away, and then returned to Joyce, laughing. Joyce continued to cry as she looked with wonder at her adopted daughter who had been so cruelly mishandled at the hands of the prison guards. After a time of silent, heartfelt communion, Cathy began to instruct her about heaven. 'The spiritual realm is our normal home, Joyce,' she told her earthly guardian. 'I chose to spend some time on earth, and I chose the body and circumstances under which that time would be spent. We were given that choice as an opportunity to grow in our love of God and to help others grow as well. You were one of my primary assignments, although I wasn't aware of it while I was on Earth.'

"'Me? You were to help me?' Joyce responded in surprise.

"'Yes. You thought it was the other way around, but I was placed into your life to help you grow in love and compassion. A big part of that growth involved your becoming more selfless in your interaction with others. But there were others with the same mission, like Earl and Sam.'"

Much as the NDE experience overlaps that of the UFO encounter, they are far from identical. There is at least one major difference as well. Whereas the UFO phenomenon quite often evokes secular, materialistic interpretations and notions of government cover-ups, there is no counterpart to these interpretations in the NDE cases, which invariably are interpreted in religious terms. Government involvement there is simply not contemplated, nor should it be. As far as I'm aware, nobody on the brink of death has been escorted to a group of bug-eyed Greys. I wouldn't reject the possibility of something like that happening, but if I ever heard of such a thing, I'd be laughing a lot.

CHAPTER TWENTY EIGHT

Angels and Greys

This chapter seeks to integrate UFO lore into a coherent Christian understanding. The integrating factor is the intersection of UFO and angelic activity.

A take-away from the elements presented earlier should include a sense that UFOs are indeed real and that the issue itself is the subject of great governmental concern. This conclusion is supported by the evidence presented in the other chapters.

A far more important conclusion that bears heeding, from the information presented throughout this commentary, is the likelihood that UFOs are intimately connected with the angelic communities associated with God and satan, and that we remove God from our lives at our very real peril. The writer of Hebrews was cited in and earlier chapter as noting that angels might well appear among us in the guise of strangers. I do know from 2 Kings 6:15-17 that angels have in the past rescued Israelites from destruction:

> "And when the servant of the man of God was risen early, and gone forth, behold, an host compassed the city, both with horses and chariots. And his servant said unto him, Alas, my master! What shall we do? And he answered, Fear not; for they who are with us are more than they who are with them. And Elisha prayed, and said, Lord, I pray thee, open his eyes, that he may see. And the Lord opened the eyes of the young man, and he saw; and, behold, the mountain was full of horses and chariots of fire around about Elisha."

The same thing happened to Gideon when the Lord told him to defeat the Midianites with only three hundred men. He did so with the help of many angels. These angelic helpers did not stop working on mankind's behalf when the Old Testament came to a close; in fact they have been out and about with their help during the many wars which Israel has been engaged in since the reinstatement of their nationhood in 1948, when a number of miraculous events associated with the 1948, 1956, 9167 and 1973 wars have been recorded. Accounts of them are available on the Internet. Scripture also strongly suggests that the war of Ezekiel 38/39 will be fought on the side of Israel by a host of angels.

For reasons that I present in Chapter Thirty One I'm convinced that angels help individuals as well via direct communication. The account in Judges 6 of the angel who spoke with Gideon is but one Scriptural example of many that continued on into New Testament times and beyond. There were multiple angelic visitations to Daniel, shielding him from grave danger and imparting important information to him. Also, angelic visitations informed Mary of her unique role in giving birth to Israel's Messiah at the Annunciation and to the shepherds at the birth of Jesus.

I've heard of some recent stories where angels have lent a hand when the going got rough. Actually, that may be far more common than we think. I have a sister-in-law, for example, who came to the Lord out of just such a situation. Faced with the forcible entrance of a man who was bent on assault, she managed, by following the instructions of a still voice inside her, to thwart his efforts. I can't say with certainty, but I suspect that angels have extracted me from many a dire situation. And if it happened to me, it can happen to you. Among those likely incidents that I remember particularly well was a motorcycle accident I was involved in during my college years. As I was heading for school one morning, a driver, distracted by the sun in her eyes, turned left in front of me. My bike hit her grille and the impact tossed me off headfirst so fast that I left my shoes behind. We didn't normally wear helmets back then, and my naked head was vulnerable, heading as it was directly for a fire hydrant. But I hit a telephone pole first, just grazing it with my chin, which was sufficient to turn me sideways into the hydrant and thus save my head and my life with it. After a week of nursing bruises, I was up and about with no ill effects. The sequence of impacts kept me from death by fractions of an inch.

Later in life my wife and I took various other trips on motorcycles, a memorable one going cross-country from the Seattle area to the Eastern seaboard. Going through North Carolina on one of the major freeways, we were next to a big old dump truck when it blew a rear tire. Shrapnel whizzed past us, but not one piece touched us. Less than an hour later, the car directly in front of us suddenly swerved to the right, exposing us to a ladder lying in the middle of the road. I live with a genetic malady called Marie-Tooth-Charkault Disease, that manifests itself in my case with exceptionally slow nerve propagation. I don't react quickly to sudden events. When I saw that ladder dead ahead, I knew that we were done for. But then something yanked hard on my handlebar, swerving me out of the way. We passed it within an inch. I *know* that the hand on the handlebar wasn't mine.

Then, of course was the time, as I had noted in my novel *Buddy* and my Christian nonfiction work *Marching to a Worthy Drummer,* when Danny, who was severely afflicted with cerebral palsy, inadvertantly placed us in a life-threatening situation by tangling his rigid arm in the flying wire of my hang glider. The situation was resolved only through fervent prayer. There were other incidents with the glider and with airplanes that I'd rather not think about, other than to thank God for the angelic support. I'd cast another terrifying memory out of my mind if I could, but I can't. I didn't think it would have been possible to have subjected my brother's ultralight to the buffeting it (and I) received in a wind shear and to have remained intact. Either God or superman brought it safely back to Earth. I'm placing my bet on God, through an angelic rescue.

Not only did some of the events have Christian implications, but also a strong linkage was found between the UFO phenomena and Judeo-Christian Scripture.

Factors within and beyond the UFO issue support the observation that we exist at a unique time in history where life as we have known it is coming to a God-ordained conclusion. We are nearing the end of two thousand years of human history following Jesus' crucifixion and resurrection on the third day. But there is another third day to contemplate – the third day of Psalm 90 and 2 Peter 3:8, the beginning of which equates to the start of the third thousand-year period since that same crucifixion, where Revelation describes Jesus' return for His millennial reign on Earth. Many Christian theologians and laypersons are convinced that we are on the very verge of the end-time scenario which includes Jesus' return.

Here's another item for contemplation: as the time of Jesus' ministry approached, two things began to happen: a sense of expectation and a sharp increase in demonic activity. Both of these harbingers of Jesus' return are now present on Earth.

We know, from the review herein of UFO activity, that the mainstream media is not trustworthy. We need not have turned to the UFO issue to have come to that conclusion. We simply could have observed that fact from the media treatment of more mundane "news" over the past several years.

More importantly, with media support aided by the poor performance, ranging from indifference to wholesale corruption, of our Churches and religious spokespersons, our government and the public as a whole have turned their backs on our Judeo-Christian God.

We must realize that the only trustworthy document in the world is the Judeo-Christian Bible, and we must turn our attention back to it and rely less on the prevailing secular presumptions and the "news" we get in the papers and on television. We must abandon not God but the secular fables that have so profoundly undermined Him.

Commonality was shown to exist between modern sightings and Scriptural references to encounters between man and other beings, and of the activities of these beings in the context of God's relationship with mankind. We have noted in Scripture a similarity between some remarkable abilities of heavenly messengers and the risen Jesus to the inexplicable attributes of UFO occupants. Finally, we have removed some of the technical mystique behind supposed visitations of UFO occupants in the ancient past by asserting a greater sophistication of earlier man than an evolutionary viewpoint would permit. But can a purpose be discerned behind the UFO visitations corresponding to the clear purposes of Biblical visitations?

I imagine, all permutations of believers and nonbelievers being at least theoretically possible, that there exists a camp of those who believe in God but not in UFOs. Is there enough reality to the sightings or the anomalies in our history to bother with the religious implications, or would it be a waste of time like many theologians think? Did Mr. Kenneth Arnold and the vast numbers of people after his 1947 sighting mistake something mundane or created by some secret government project for some spectacular new device, or did they actually see something from beyond our notion of time and space?

Scripture, according to our earlier review of Biblical UFO encounters argues rather eloquently for the religious implications of UFO encounters. There is, in fact, so much overlap between the two subjects that such views cannot logically be separated. Therefore, it would seem reasonable to assert that if faith in Scripture does not demand a corresponding acknowledgment of the existence of UFOs, and specifically that their manifestations represent angelic visitations, it at least rather strongly hints of this possibility.

Because the Christian God, being man's Creator, is anything but an alien being, the Christian UFO buff enjoys a much more benign outlook concerning UFO occupants: in an angelic context, such beings might be either good or evil, as both types are found in the Bible; however, both types are also under the control of God.

If some Christians frown upon UFOs, perhaps the media might be to blame as I have alluded to above. Over at least the past forty or fifty years, the media in the United States has engaged in a three-pronged attempt to discredit UFO sightings: marginalizing those who have sighted the objects as credulous, easily-influenced and emotionally unbalanced; furnishing (im)perfectly mundane explanations for the sighting events; and, in line with the purely materialistic outlook, emphasizing the physical impossibility of the maneuvers claimed for them.

Regarding the marginalization issue, we note that the media (and, horrifyingly, our own government) is becoming so blatant about that tactic, especially for those who do not subscribe to the "official" political, economic or religious views, and increasingly for the Christian community, that it is both easy to recognize the lies for what they are and their effect in marginalizing Christians. Several decades ago when Christians were in the center of mainstream society, they might have lost some status as members of the UFO camp. Now they have nothing to lose, which is where God would have them anyway. If one is tempted to argue the point, he should first refer to Matthew 5 and First Corinthians 1.

As for the commonplace explanations for the sighting events, we immediately think of the case of Dr. J. Allen Hynek, a physicist who was hired by the Air Force's Project Bluebook staff for the specific purpose of creating those mundane explanations. Enthusiastic at the beginning about his role, he was the one who came up with the famous 'swamp gas' theory to explain away many of the UFO incidents. He eventually wearied of his task, finally coming to the realization that while his explanations might be satisfactory for some people, they weren't so hot for him. Much to the embarrassment of the Air Force, he went over to the UFO camp as a firm believer. As we have shown earlier, other 'explanations', most notably the 'weather balloon', have been exposed as outright lies.

The spectacular maneuvers claimed by many of those who have witnessed UFOs do indeed appear to violate the laws governing the motion of large physical objects – for those bodies subject to our dimensional restrictions. Actually, in performing these maneuvers, the UFOs appear to exhibit some characteristics of quantum mechanics, which have been observed for objects in the atomic domain. Having been observed in actuality, these characteristics, while certainly being counter-intuitive and in violation of the known laws governing larger objects, cannot be dismissed as impossible. Interestingly, Jesus exhibited some of these same characteristics prior to His crucifixion by eluding those who attempted to kill Him and suddenly; appearing to His disciples, and after His resurrection, as noted in John 20:19-29 by passing through walls and yet feeling solid to those who touched Him.

A fact that can be readily extracted from the summaries of modern UFO incidents is that most of the overt investigations, including those performed by the government, have a crucial deficiency. The investigators didn't perform a follow-up after the event. Most sighting reports discuss only the data relevant to the immediate occurrence, while ignoring the possible long-term impact on the individual witness. In those cases where the witness did describe a related long term impact, this aspect of the event was recorded only because the witness sought medical help and was willing to share the experience. In virtually all these cases, the impact was so significant as to be life-changing.

Another glaring deficiency in virtually all of the investigations to date is the entry assumption that whatever these beings are, they are of a uniform nature. If there is any one commonality in the variety of sighting reports that stands out it is their lack of commonality, in that many reports seem to be at odds with others with respect to both their nature and their intent. This very difference of itself suggests one quite important possibility: the UFO occupants themselves may be of at least two very different camps, one being benign and the other hostile. The notion of opposing camps, in turn, evokes the Biblical image of angelic beings, one group under God and the other under Satan, at war with each other. Biblical references to this situation abound, an example being found in Revelation 12:7-9:

> "And there was war in heaven: Michael and his angels fought against the dragon; and the dragon fought and his angels, And prevailed not; neither was their place found any more in heaven. And the great dragon was cast out, that old serpent, called the Devil, and Satan, which deceiveth the whole world: he was cast out into the earth, and his angels were cast out with him."

There you have it – at least my take on it: UFO occupants are angels on two very different missions, one to serve God as He moves on behalf of mankind, and the other to impede Him in a hostile effort to destroy humanity. So then, what *is* the end game?

I would suggest that at the present time we who reside in the material domain are in a large schoolroom, where we're learning at a painfully slow rate how to love. It is only when each of us has acquired the ability through our companion acquisition of selflessness to love others without reservation that we have then achieved God's desire for us. At that point, love wins and we have played out His end game for us.

CHAPTER TWENTY NINE

The Reality of UFO Encounters

Many Christians believe in the existence of UFOs and consider their occupants to be spiritual in nature. However, a majority of these perceive them in a negative light, considering them to be of satanic origin. A number of Christian leaders have been outspoken about this, having in the past addressed and now continue to speak to large audiences on the UFO topic. When they do, they almost invariably describe the phenomenon as demonic, and issue warnings to their fellows against any association with them. More than one popular speaker has gone so far as to advise his audience that any person who has been in contact with a UFO occupant to pray for the deliverance of his soul. Popular theologian Chuck Missler, for example, favors angelic beings as the source of UFO contacts, as do I. As this highly-respected Christian scholar noted on page 324 of his 1997 book *Alien Encounters,* co-authored by Mark Eastman,

"Demonic access of any kind requires the lowering of the gate of one's will. This can be initiated by a subtle "entry" – involvement in a seemingly "harmless" pursuit or game such as a "ouija" board, a séance, a party game, or something more serious. This can make you prey for the forces of darkness and eligible for the types of events or pseudo-events described in this book."

Again, on page 326, he makes this dire warning:

> "If you see a UFO, immediately call on God and plead His blood as your basis for immunity. And don't let yourself become hypnotized. It's serious business. Your eternal destiny is at stake."

Some might view Dr. Missler as appearing to focus exclusively on the side of the fallen angel, rather than acknowledging commentary found throughout Scripture that angels exist in both unfallen and fallen states. Many contemporary theologians who address the UFO issue concur with Dr. Missler on this point. Yet, can you imagine what Gideon would have done about the angel sitting under the tree if he had held this point of view? Would he have run away and prayed to God to keep his soul intact? Would he have complained to his father? Or how about Mary? Would she have told Gabriel that she didn't want anybody fooling around with her body, particularly her reproductive system, and to get the heck away from her? It was noted earlier that the Bible describes many other encounters with beings that the Judeo-Christian community accepts as having been angelic, but would describe as alien in a more modern setting.

I count myself among those who respect Dr. Missler. Many of his insights into Scripture are unique to him and quite interesting. I don't play with ouija boards, as I happen to agree with him on that matter. I also agree with him regarding the possibility of demonic influence – on some UFO encounters. But I don't think that's the entire story. I see UFOs as related to angelic activity. We know from Genesis 6 and elsewhere that some angels wrought evil. On the other hand, we also know from Matthew 26 and elsewhere that there are good angels as well. Paul, in 1 Corinthians 6:3 alludes to the existence of both good and bad angels:

> *"Know ye not that we shall judge angels? How much more things that pertain to this life?"*

For that reason, unless he has mitigated his stance against UFOs in statements that I have missed reading, I respectfully take issue with Dr. Missler's apparent across-the-board negativity regarding them. If he indeed is not completely negative regarding the phenomenon, I apologize to him and to the reader. Dr. Missler's works are well worth reading regardless of that issue.

In opposition to an uncompromising negativity regarding the UFO phenomenon, I could cite my own UFO experience that occurred when I was not a Christian, which turned me toward Christianity rather than away from it. Furthermore, any contact that I might have had with a UFO occupant was completely involuntary. I think my God is big enough to keep me out of trouble all on His own, although I agree with Dr. Missler that dabbling in the occult, a voluntary act, is a real no-no. I also agree with him that the world will encounter, and perhaps already has entered, a time of spiritual depravity, false doctrine, and a massive effort originating in the spiritual realm to mislead. This view is supported by the numerous warnings of Jesus and Paul, particularly in Matthew 24, Romans, Timothy, Thessalonians and Revelation, regarding the spiritual darkness that will be visited upon the human race as the Church Age draws to a close.

The bad feelings of many popular Christian spokespersons toward UFO encounters might include the secular notions that UFO occupants are alien to us and are frighteningly superior, but their greatest concern probably relates to the Bible account in Genesis 6:2-4, which claims that some sons of God, which usually are interpreted as fallen angels, intermarried with human women, producing people of enormous stature and polluting the human bloodline in a possible attempt to pollute the specific bloodline that would lead to Jesus. Confronted with that situation and its attendant violence, God vowed to destroy the Earth and all its inhabitants, save Noah and his family, after the passage of one hundred twenty years.

Many evangelical theologians directly associate the Great Flood of Noah with God's desire to cleanse the earth of these hybrid beings and their disobedient angelic fathers and terminate the violence that they wrought on our planet. The odd creatures are considered evil for a number of reasons: their disobedience toward God in leaving their assigned heavenly station and mingling with the inhabitants of Earth; their forbidden sexual lust which led to their intrusion upon the exclusive earthly relationship between human males and human females as established by God; and the untimely knowledge that they imparted to humans, which interfered with the sequence of events which God had planned for us.

The term "sons of God", by which the Bible describes these beings who produced hybrids, readily identifies them as angels. Their evil nature is described elsewhere in Scripture, particularly in Revelation 12:7-13:

"And there was war in heaven; Michael and his angels fought against the dragon, and the dragon fought, and his angels, and prevailed not, neither was their place found any more in heaven. And the great dragon was cast out, that old serpent, called the devil and satan, who deceiveth the whole world; he was cast out into the earth, and his angels were cast out with him.

"And I heard a loud voice saying in heaven, Now is come salvation, and strength, and the kingdom of our God, and the power of his Christ; for the accuser of our brethren is cast down, who accused them before our God day and night. And they overcame him by the blood of the Lamb, and by the word of their testimony; and they loved not

their lives unto the death. Therefore rejoice, ye heavens, and ye that dwell in them. Woe to the inhabitants of the earth and of the sea! For the devil is come down unto you, having great wrath, because he knoweth that he hath but a short time.

"And when the dragon saw that he was cast unto the earth, he persecuted the woman who brought forth the male child."

Here again bad angels are depicted. But note that there are two camps in this drama, and one of these camps consists of good angels. When the topic of UFOs is addressed by Evangelical theologians, they almost uniformly link the UFO experience with angels, but they tend to forget about the good ones. This oversight is difficult to understand, given the numerous instances in Scripture, like Gabriel's discussion with Daniel in Daniel Chapter 9, and his later Annunciation to Mary in Luke 1, where Gabriel obviously is serving God in obedience and interacting quite benignly with humans.

Nevertheless, the Bible makes it plain that there are fallen angels who behave with evil intent toward humans. Both Chuck Missler and Scott Alan Roberts address the offspring of these fallen angels as Nephilim. According to Roberts in his 2012 book *The Rise and Fall of the Nephilim,*

"Some Christian ufologists, such as Chuck Missler, appear to believe that the "Sons of God" in Genesis 6:2 are actually extra-terrestrials or grey aliens, and that these beings are actually fallen angels or demons that have appeared during the antediluvian times in order to genetically alter the human race, and to pollute the bloodline of Jesus. Thus, the Nephilim would be the hybrid race of these beings in this view."

Roberts also claims that the fallen angels, fathers of the nephilim, belonged to the caste of the "watchers" that were so briefly and enigmatically mentioned in Jeremiah 4:16 and Daniel 4:13, 17, and 23:

"Make mention to the nations; behold, publish against Jerusalem, that watchers come over from a far country, and give out their voice against the cities of Judah."

"I [Nebudchadnezzar] saw in the visions of my head upon my bed, and, behold, a watcher and an holy one came down from heaven; . . .This matter is by decree of the watchers, and the demand by the word of the holy ones, to the intent that the living may know that the Most High ruleth in the kingdom of men, and giveth it to whomsoever He will, and setteth up over it the basest of men. . .And

whereas the king saw a watcher and an holy one coming down from heaven, and saying, Hew the tree down, and destroy it; yet leave the stump of its roots in the earth, even with a band of iron and brass, in the tender grass of the field; and let him be wet with the dew of heaven, and let his portion be with the beasts of the field, till seven times pass over him;"

In his Chapter 5, entitled "The Watchers", Roberts turns to the extra-canonical Book of Enoch to glean further information about the watchers and the Nephilim. The Book of Enoch, fragments of which were found among the Dead Sea Scrolls, described these beings in greater detail. As noted above with regard to the angels of Revelation 12, if the watchers indeed are angels, there were both good and bad ones, the bad watchers being the fallen angels who abandoned their assigned heavenly station to cohabit with human women. The disobedient watchers, Roberts notes, had angered God on a number of levels, including their disobedience to God, their impartation of knowledge prematurely to humans, and their having had sexual liaisons with women, thus polluting the human DNA, which threatened the bloodline to Jesus as well as violating God's intent to limit marriage to a human male and a human female. Roberts quotes several passages from Enoch, i.e. 1 Enoch 7:10, 11-14, 9:5-14, 10:12 and 13, and 18-20 that are descriptive of the watchers' malfeasance. These passages include the following, where the watcher Azazyel figures prominently as a target for epithets:

"Then they took wives, each choosing for himself' whom they began to approach, and with whom they cohabitated; teaching them sorcery, incantations. . ."

"And the women conceiving brought forth giants, whose stature was each three hundred cubits. These devoured all which the labor of men produced; until it became impossible to feed them; when they turned themselves against men, in order to devour them; and began to injure birds, beasts, reptiles, and fishes, to eat their flesh one after another, and to drink their blood."

"Thou hast seen what Azazyel has done, how he has taught every species of iniquity upon earth, and has disclosed to the world all the secret things which are done in the heavens. Shamyaza also has taught sorcery, to whom thou hast given authority over those who are associated with him. They have gone together to the daughters of men; have lain with them; have become polluted; and have discovered crimes to them. The women likewise have brought forth giants. Thus has the whole earth been filled with blood and with iniquity. And now behold the souls of those who are dead, cry out. And complain even to the gate of heaven. Their groaning ascends; nor can they escape from the unrighteousness which is committed on earth. Thou knowest all things, before they exist. Thou knowest these things, and what has been done by them; yet thou dost not speak to us. What on account of these things ought we to do to them?"

"All the earth has been corrupted by the effects of the teaching of Azazyel. To him therefore ascribe the whole crime. To Gabriel also the Lord said, Go to the biters, to the reprobates, to the children of fornication; and destroy the children of fornication, the offspring of the Watchers, from among men; bring them forth, and excite them one against another. Let them perish by mutual slaughter; for length of days shall not be theirs"

"Destroy all the souls addicted to dalliance, and the offspring of the Watchers, for they have tyrannized over mankind. Let every oppressor perish from the face of the earth; let every evil work be destroyed."

Roberts makes an interesting connection between the watchers and a famous modern UFO event. He notes that in the occult science of numerology the number of 33 denotes the highest level of human consciousness, which is echoed in the hierarchy of Freemasonry where the 33rd degree is the highest order. He comments further that Israel's Mount Hermon was the location on the 33rd parallel where the fallen watchers arrived on Earth, and proceeds from there to point out that on the other side of the world from Israel the famous alleged 1947 UFO crash occurred at Roswell, New Mexico, also on the 33rd parallel. He seems to indicate that Roswell is precisely on the opposite side of the Earth from Mount Hermon, but if one traces the two locations on a globe, they don't quite line up on opposite sides. Yet, they are somewhat close to doing so.

On page 98 of *The Rise and Fall of the Nephilim,* Roberts makes a perceptive statement. He claims that people tend to interpret ancient documents, particularly religious ones, as mythical and so to dismiss them as essentially irrelevant to our lives. We do so, he asserts, in order to perceive ourselves as intellectually superior to our ancestors, whom we view as naïve, superstitious, and engaging in outmoded ways of thinking. But perhaps, he speculates, our own scientifically-oriented way of thinking is too sterile. Maybe some of those ancient "myths" contain real truths, which we ignore to our disadvantage. I wholeheartedly agree with Roberts' opinion here, but I would go farther, by reminding Christians that both Peter and Paul (2 Peter 1:20, 21 and 2 Timothy 3:16 and 17) claimed that all Scripture was inspired by the Holy Spirit and should be considered truthful in its entirety. It has often been the case that these statements have caused me to persist beyond an initial misunderstanding of Scripture, where others have been tempted to cast the same aside as either mythical or in error, to the acquisition of valuable insights regarding the nature of God.

CHAPTER THIRTY

The Richness of My Encounter

From my perspective, the most important take-away from my memory of the event is that, most happily, some UFO encounters have a positive flavor supportive of Christianity and its foundational Scripture and are recognized as such by the Christians who are involved.

A slim minority of Christians view the UFO phenomenon as both real and positive without ruling out the possibility that some UFO experiences might fall into the negative category. We – and I include myself among them, having had my own UFO experience with very positive long-range consequences – perceive UFO contacts in terms of angelic visitations. We acknowledge the existence of both obedient and fallen angels, which accounts for the variety of contact experiences, particularly the extremes of good and bad.

The reality of my personal UFO experience was verified more by the aftermath of the experience than the actual event itself. That's not unusual, as many accounts of interactions with UFOs describe persistent effects arising from one-time encounters. Most of these effects involve fear of some sort, even terror, and that's what makes my encounter different – a complete absence of fear. If anything, I felt more of a kinship with whoever occupied the craft that I saw. That positivity places me in a rare category of contemporary individuals, but I'm not completely alone. Another positive account, and one involving God as well, is described in Chapter Twenty Four regarding the incident on the journey from London to Stratford.

I qualify the rarity of my category with the word "contemporary", because there is one source of past experiences on the positive side of the ledger. That source is the Bible, and accounts there having the same implications as my event are anything but rare. Interestingly, the other contemporary person of whom I am aware who had a positive experience also reported Christian implications. My own UFO experience was intensely Christian as well, and it was a deep one which imparted knowledge that, as far as I know, was unique to me. It also changed my life. But I was uncertain for many years as to whether I was merely a witness to a sighting event, or if my involvement was deeper than that.

I made no connection at the time between the sighting and God, and for good reason. I was brought up to consider Christians to be superstitious malcontents who needed God for a crutch. My family was intellectually-oriented and had no need for myths. With all the scoffing and laughingly snide remarks our parents had made over the years regarding the personal weakness of Christians and the irrelevance of Christianity to normal life we got the message loud and clear: well-adjusted people don't indulge in religious nonsense. At the time I knew nothing about God, nor did I want to. I was perfectly content to leave God entirely out of my life.

The UFO experience didn't open anything up to me – not then. In fact, I forgot about it shortly afterwards. When something very strange like that happens, one tends to wonder whether it was real or a hallucination, and shove it into the back of his mind. At least that's what I did. At the time I was having a lot on my plate, too. I didn't think again about the UFO until maybe six or more years later. By that time, I'd changed jobs and even forgot the name of my traveling companion. I still can't remember his name, and it frustrates me, because I'd really like to compare notes with him.

But in the meantime I had become a Christian - maybe six months after the UFO sighting and with no outside input, I suddenly had a yearning to read the Bible. During that time, I made no connection between that experience and the UFO. It was only several years later when talking to another person about how I became a Christian that I made the connection – and it hit me like concrete dropping from a collapsing building. After that I began to revisit the event and explore the notion that my experience embraced more than just a sighting.

I continue to experience vague memories of a conversation, during which highlights of my future were given in a compassionate, even loving, framework. The things that happened afterward seem to have enabled me to grow toward the selflessness that God would cherish. These foretold significant times included a very dark period during which I would experience a profound grief, but my life was to end well – in fact, very well. I seem to remember that immediately after the event I was wishing that the forecast grief period would be over and I'd be experiencing a much more benign aftermath.

The period of grief did indeed occur, and now I've passed beyond that stage into a much happier time. But other things have also happened that reinforce the possibility that I actually had contact with the occupants of the craft. The most important of these is the informational aspect. I possessed information of which I had no previous interest or understanding; moreover this information appears to be unique to me. A portion of this information required little effort on my part, other than to read Scripture. Upon the reading, I seem to have been given the ability, quite uncharacteristic of me, to read passages and quickly integrate them into related passages and to the general body of Scripture. For other information I was given a strong desire to receive it, but the acquisition itself required much work and persistence on my part.

The most important information of this kind resulted from an unexpectedly urgent desire to work out the arithmetic details of Jesus' feeding of the multitudes as I describe in Chapter Nineteen. The answer was a long time in coming, about ten years involving much frustration, confusion and uncertainty, but eventually resulted in a precise knowledge of the numbers associated with the feedings, such as the number of fragments per basket of leftovers, and the exact patterns by which the multitudes were fed. The final result was an enormous surprise – the patterns of the feedings combined to form a cross, as I describe in Part 5 of my book *Family of God*, Appendix 2 of my book *Marching to a Worthy Drummer*, and in my novel *Cathy*. As far as I know, this information is unique. Other information was given to me that, although not unique, is quite rare and of a nature that resides far beyond the information available in the usual Church setting. I share that information in the books noted above, as well as in my other novels *Buddy, Jacob* and *Home, Sweet Heaven.*

Of the knowledge that I was given, the head portion was less important than that of the heart. It also involved more than a little humor. A compassion for the handicapped was instilled in me, leading me to volunteer at a local nursing home. The activity began as a Bible study, which, in turn, led to a companionship with a young man who was severely afflicted with cerebral palsy. That, in turn, led to adventures that I wouldn't have dreamed of in my pre-Christian life. I recall those adventures, both scary and humorous, in my novel *Buddy*, in my nonfiction work *Marching to a Worthy Drummer* and in Chapter Eight herein as well. My life after the grief period has been rich and joyful indeed and I wouldn't change it for the world, which makes the precursor UFO event, on balance, a very positive experience. Not only that, but the knowledge and adventures that my Christianity has endowed me with gives me a firm faith, which translates into a positive outlook on my ultimate future despite my forced participation in an ever more darkening and chaotic world.

Given the nature of the experience that I had and its correlation with similar accounts in Scripture, I lean heavily toward an explanation of the beings associated with UFOs as angelic, both obedient and fallen. I happen to be one of the fortunate ones who encountered a good angelic presence. I appreciate that this attribution doesn't square with the physicality of the Roswell incident, with its remains of both craft and occupants. I don't have an answer for that, except to acknowledge that perhaps our physical universe is large enough to accommodate more than one sentient species, and that the spiritual domain inhabited by God and His angels presides over all such species, human and other-worldly. I see nothing in the Bible that would contradict such an arrangement.

Chapter Thirty One

Putting the Pieces Together

In the previous chapters on the topic of angels, I've focused for the most part on their interaction with us and aspects of their nature as interpreted by the world at large. In this chapter I'll present my own opinion of who they are, and of how I see them as fitting into the Family of God.

Given the femininity of the Holy Spirit, the identification of the Holy Trinity as a divine Family is readily understandable. The functional differentiation of the three Members is also straightforward in that context, with the Father assuming the role of Divine Will, the Holy Spirit as the Divine Means, and the Son Jesus Christ as the Divine Reality.

The family structure of the Trinity also brings the Genesis account of the creation of man into focus as a reprise of the development of the Trinity itself. Specifically, the creation of man in the image of God in Genesis 1:26 and 27 elaborates on our understanding of God, particularly of His gendered plurality:

> *"And God said, Let us make man in our image, after our likeness; and let them have dominion over the fish of the sea, and over the fowl of the air, and over the cattle, and over all the earth, and over every creeping thing that creepeth upon the earth. So God created man in his own image, in the image of God created he him; male and female created he them."*

In that same vein, the account in Genesis 2 of the creation of Eve out of Adam may reprise the selfless nobility of the Father in His extraction of the Holy Spirit from Himself as a separate Entity, which automatically reduced His own status from that of All-in-All to a Member of a Holy Partnership. In that holy union, the Father reclaimed the Holy Spirit in love rather than in the original arrangement of ownership within Himself. Thus the story of the creation of Eve harks back to an even greater drama which took place in an earlier age:

> *"And the Lord God said, it is not good that the man should be alone; I will make him an help fit for him. . . And the Lord God caused a deep sleep to fall upon Adam, and he slept; and he took one of his ribs, and closed up the flesh instead thereof; and the rib, which the Lord God had taken from man, made he a woman, and brought her unto the man.*

> *"And Adam said, this is now bone of my bones, and flesh of my flesh; she shall be called Woman, because she was taken out of Man. Therefore shall a man leave his father and his mother, and shall cleave unto his wife; and they shall be one flesh."*

In Chapter 5 of my novel *Buddy* I had made that connection between this account of the creation of Eve and the separation of the Holy Sprit from the Father. In that passage, the Holy Spirit converses with Earl:

> "Earl," She continued presently, "Jesus and I were always part of the Father, but at the very beginning there was no separation. We existed together as One, and that One was the Father, the Divine Will. Being alone and in full command of Himself, He had the choice to remain in that state and retain within Himself absolute power and authority over everything that He would subsequently create." A tear leaked out from her eye. She dabbed at it with a finger.

> "But then," she said, regaining control over her emotions, "the Father did something that was the essence of selflessness. It was of an order of nobility that transcends everything that came after."

> "Even Jesus on the cross?" he asked in wonder. "That was pretty painful. And humbling."

> "Yes. Even that. The Father was first to humble Himself. He set the standard. And yes, it was painful too. Remember that

He possessed everything that was and ever will be. He chose to give that up."

"What did He do?"

"He chose to create an Other out of Himself, giving up part of Himself in the process and restricting His portion in everything that is or ever will be to that of one Member of a Partnership. He decided to share His exalted position with that Other. But here's the great beauty of what he did: in relinquishing His singleness He added love into the mix. And through this love He again became One with His Other."

Note here that the Holy Spirit appears to Earl as an individual Woman. I had always pictured the Holy Spirit in that way, although I recognized that this appearance couldn't begin to encompass the enormity of Her being. I did address that incongruity in Chapter 7 of *Buddy*, but all-too briefly, as my mind couldn't grasp it to the point of satisfying both the reader and myself.

"You call yourself Wisdom. Are you really the Holy Spirit?"

"Well, actually, I'm a little more extensive than what you see, being God and all, but the me that you see is a manifestation, so, yes, to you I am."

"I'm honored. But how do you find the time to visit me personally, me being just one among billions. I'd think we'd look like ants to you."

She laughed. "That's something that Alicia knows but you'll have to wait to find out. Let's just say that it's a God thing. I came to confirm what you suspected, Earl. I'll be running along now. See you soon."

Turning to another account in the Bible of God's plan for mankind, it can be seen in Ephesians 5:31 and 32 in Paul's forecast of God's ultimate intent for man a sharp differentiation between the individual and the collective entity the Church. Here we see in this mystery of Paul's that the Church will marry Christ in the context of Eve's marriage to Adam:

"For this cause shall a man leave his father and mother, and shall be joined unto his wife, and they two shall be one flesh. This is a great mystery, but I speak concerning Christ and the Church."

Not only is it a mystery, but a profound one indeed, and on several levels. On the level of man, Paul's use of Adam's statement in Genesis 2 regarding marriage identifies the Church's marriage to Christ as a functional, fully-gendered one, with procreation as the inevitable outcome, as Paul emphasizes in Romans 7:4:

"Wherefore, my brethren, ye also are become dead to the law by the body of Christ, that ye should be married to another, even to him who is raised from the dead, that we should bring forth fruit unto God."

At this point the objection might be raised that we are genderless in our spiritual form as also noted by Paul in Galatians 3:28:

"There is neither Jew nor Greek, there is neither bond nor free, there is neither male nor female; for ye are all one in Christ Jesus."

The resolution of this apparent dichotomy is as straightforward as understanding the distinction between the individual and the collective. As individuals, spiritual man doesn't participate in gendered activities any more than an arm or a foot or a clavicle does. The function of gender is allocated to the collective Church as a fully-gendered woman, just as a human woman is gendered only in her entirety. Paul goes to great pains to make this point, as in 1 Corinthians 12:4-20:

"Now there are diversities of gifts, but the same Spirit. And there are differences of administrations, but the same Lord. And there are diversities of operations, but it is the same God who worketh all in all. But the manifestation of the Spirit is given to every man to profit.

"For to one is given, by the Spirit, the word of wisdom; to another, the word of knowledge by the same Spirit; to another, faith by the same Spirit; to another, the gifts of healing by the same Spirit; to another, the working of miracles; to another, prophecy; to another, discerning of spirits; to another, various kinds of tongues; to another, the interpretation of tongues. But all these worketh that one and the very same Spirit, dividing to every man severally as [She] will.

"For as the body is one, and hath many members, and all the members of that one body, being many, are one body, so also is Christ. For by one Spirit were we all baptized into on e body, whether we be Jews or Greeks, whether we be bond or free; and have been all made to drink into one Spirit. For the body is not one member, but many. If the foot shall say, Because I am not the eye, I am not of the body; is it, therefore, not of the body? And if the ear shall say, Because I am not the eye, I am not of the body; is it, therefore, not of the body? If the whole body were an eye, where were the hearing? If the whole were hearing, where were the smelling? But now hath God set the members, every one of them, in the body, as it hath pleased him. And if they were all one member, where were the body? But now are they many members, yet but one body."

Just as King David represented the Holy Father in Psalms, so did his son King Solomon represent the Holy Spirit in Proverbs. It is my opinion, and just that, that the Psalms and Proverbs were intended as instructions to the Jesus to come in the flesh from His Holy Father and Mother. Regardless, Solomon was given divine wisdom in abundance for asking for it in a selfless manner. Many Christians, upon reading 1 Kings 11:3, shoot out the lip at Solomon's many loves, considering it to be an impudent mockery of God's intent for a one man/ one woman lifelong relationship.

"And [Solomon] had seven hundred wives, princesses, and three hundred concubines; and his wives turned away his heart."

I have a more benign picture of this act of his – I see Solomon, in the abundance of his understanding of God, the Trinity, and God's plan for mankind, as foreseeing Christ's marriage to the multi-component Church. In that context, I see Solomon as attempting to represent the risen Jesus in this forecast of Jesus' marriage to the Church, wherein his many wives and concubines represented the diverse nature of the Church. Perhaps he went too far, and perhaps he did ignore God's intent of a one woman/one man marriage, but I believe that his own intent was pure in this matter.

As for the obvious distinction in Scripture between the individuals comprising the Church and its collective identity as a gendered entity, Jesus in Matthew 22: 29 and 30 wraps it up in a neat package:

"Jesus answered and said unto them, Ye do err, not knowing the scriptures, not the power of God. For in the resurrection, they neither

marry, nor are given in marriage, but are like the angels of God in heaven."

Here Jesus says essentially the same thing as Paul did in Galatians 3:28: spiritual humans may be genderless as individuals. But note that in this context that Jesus speaks of the power of God, not the lack of it. The absence of gender in the spiritual realm would represent weakness rather than strength, of something missing rather than an attribute.

But it is Jesus' last phrase in this passage that ties it all together and explains precisely where angels fit into God's grand scheme:

". . . but are like the angels of heaven."

Here again Jesus implies that God's plan for mankind is a reprise of the Trinity itself, in which the individual angels are components of a much greater Entity, the feminine Holy Spirit. Just like the situation with the composite Church, angels are seen as elements of God. In this understanding, I finally see a resolution of the gloss-over in *Buddy* that I gave of the Holy Spirit who I saw as an individual Being. Perhaps in the spiritual realm the communication among individuals is so perfect that in seeing what I would now call an angel I was actually seeing what my limited mind could see of the Holy Spirit Herself.

EPILOGUE

As an elderly man who supposedly has paid his dues to God and country, I write these final words of my story in the hope that it's not yet over - that I will still have dues to pay. Not that I'm not happy. I'm exceedingly so, thanking God daily for the opportunities that He has given me for serving Him, and on top of that, for His having so generously blessed me with a beautiful wife, both physically and spiritually, children to be proud of, and exceedingly beautiful surroundings here in the Northwest – truly God's own country. But I feel too young yet to be out of the fray. Being way too old to re-enlist, I find myself thinking with nostalgia of my brief career as a youth in the Marine Corps, wondering if I should have stayed in. Had I done that, I most certainly would have gone to Vietnam with the cream of my generation. The odds are pretty good that I would have ended my life over there.

But, had God intervened earlier under those very different circumstances, I would have died well.

Perhaps I still will die well. Our country, being laden down with corruption, appears to be entering a time of darkness, possibly to the extent of morphing into a full-blown tyranny. In this time of trouble that extends far beyond the current public perception it no longer matters which side of the political aisle one chooses to support. We're past that now, having moved beyond redemption when we muscled our Judeo-Christian God out of our public and private lives. As more than one of our forefathers forewarned us, our unique brand of representative democracy requires a godly nation to work. Now it's untenable, leaving us with the inevitability of moving into an alternate form of government, one that certainly will be more darkly repressive.

Had we been more Biblically literate, we would have been forewarned as well by the historical literature in the Bible. The Books of Samuel, Kings and Chronicles (as well as Deuteronomy and a host of other passages scattered throughout the Old and New Testaments) furnish ample warning of what happens to a people who abandon their God. It's not pretty.

Be not deceived: God may have been suppressed in America, but He's still very much alive and in control of our world, just as He was in the days of the evil kings of Israel who came after Solomon, and the evil kings of Judah a few generations later.

In Matthew 12:48, Jesus had cut some slack for those people who knew little of God:

> *"But he that knew not, and did commit things worthy of stripes, shall be beaten with few stripes. For unto whomsoever much is given, of him shall be much required; and to whom men have committed much, of him they will ask the more."*

But America, like Israel, has been given much by our Judeo-Christian God. Like Israel, America from its first founding has had a particularly intimate relationship with Him. That relationship didn't come without cost. The severity of God's warning in Deuteronomy 28:15-48 applies to us in the same manner in which it applied to Israel, and for them was historically fulfilled to the letter:

> *"But it shall come to pass, if thou wilt not hearken unto the voice of the Lord thy God, to observe to do all his commandments and his statutes which I command thee this day, that all these curses shall come upon thee, and overtake thee. Cursed shall thou be in the city, and cursed shalt thou be in the field. Cursed shall be thy basket and thy kneading-trough. Cursed shall be the fruit of thy body, and the fruit of thy land, the increase of thy cattle and the flocks of thy sheep. Cursed shall thou be when thou comest in, and cursed shalt thou be when thou goest out. The Lord shall send upon thee cursing, vexation, and rebuke, in all that thou settest thine hand to do, until thou be destroyed, and until thou perish quickly, because of the wickedness of thy doings whereby thou hast forsaken me.*

> *"The Lord shall make the pestilence cling unto thee, until he have consumed thee from off the land, to which thou goest to possess it. The Lord shall smite thee with a consumption, and with a fever, and with an and with an inflammation, and with an extreme burning, and with the sword, and with blight, and with mildew; and they shall pursue thee until thou perish. And the heaven that is over thy head shall be brass, and the earth that is under thee shall be iron. The Lord*

shall make the rain of thy land powder and dust; from heaven shall it come down upon thee, until thou be destroyed.

"The Lord shall cause thee to be smitten before thy enemies; thou shalt go out one way against them, and flee seven ways before them, and shalt be removed into all the kingdoms of the earth. And thy carcass shall be food unto all fowls of the air, and unto the beasts of the earth, and no man shall drive them away. The Lord shall smite thee with the boil of Egypt, and with the tumors, and with the scab, and with the itch, whereof thou canst not be healed. The Lord shall smite thee with madness, and blindness, and astonishment of heart; and thou shalt grope at noonday as the blind gropeth in darkness, and thou shalt not prosper in thy ways, and thou shalt be only oppressed and spoiled evermore, and no man shall save thee. Thou shalt betroth a wife, and another man shall lie with her; thou shalt build an house, and thou shalt not dwell therein; thou shalt plant a vineyard, and shalt not gather the grapes thereof. Thine ox shall be slain before thine eyes, and thou shalt not eat thereof; thine ass shall be violently taken away from before thy face, and shall not be restored to thee; thy sheep shall be given unto thine enemies, and thou shalt have none to rescue them.

"Thy sons and thy daughters shall be given unto another people, and thine eyes shall look, and fail with longing for them all the day long; and there shall be no might in thy hand. The fruit of thy land, and all thy labors, shall a nation whom thou knowest not eat up, and thou shalt be only oppressed and crushed always. So that thou shalt be mad for the sight of thine eyes which thou shalt see. The Lord shall smite thee in the knees, and in the legs, with a sore boil that cannot be healed, from the sole of thy foot unto the top of thy head. The Lord shall bring thee, and thy king whom thou shalt set over thee, unto a nation whom neither thou nor thy fathers have known, and there shalt thou serve other gods, wood and stone. And thou shalt become an astonishment, a proverb, and a byword among all nations to which the Lord shall lead thee. Thou shalt carry much seed out into the field, and shalt gather but little in; for the locust shall consume it. Thou shalt plant vineyards, and dress them, but shalt neither drink of the wine, nor gather the grapes; for the worms shall eat them. Thou shalt have olive trees throughout all thy borders, but thou shalt not anoint thyself with the oil; for thine olive shall cast its fruit. Thou shalt beget sons and daughters, but thou shalt not enjoy them; for they

shall go into captivity. All thy tgrees and fruit of thy land shall the locust consume. The stranger who is within thee shall get up above thee very high, and thou shalt come down very low. He shall lend to thee, and thou shalt not lend to him; he shall be the head, and thou shalt be the tail.

"Moreover, all these curses shall come upon thee, and shall pursue thee, and overtake thee, till thou be destroyed, because thou hearkenedst not unto the voice of the Lord thy God, to keep his commandments and his statutes which he commanded thee. And they shall be upon thee for a sign and for a wonder, and upon thy seed forever. Because thou servedst not the Lord thy God with joyfulness, and with gladness of heart, for the abundance of all things, therefore shalt thou serve thine enemies whom the Lord shall send against thee, in hunger and in thirst, and in nakedness, and in want of all things; and he shall put a yoke of iron upon thy neck, until he have destroyed thee."

Whew! It's so much easier to read these words when one thinks that they apply to someone else. But we ourselves have shared in the intimacy of God as did the people of Israel and Judah. And, alas, of all the evil deeds done by them and written in the Books of Kings and Chronicles, we have done the same in our complacent indifference toward God, and more besides. If they deserved the wrath of God, we deserve yet more.

Yet, the stressful times ahead will provide us with a unique opportunity to serve God. Our persevering Christian faith will shine brightly out of the coming darkness, drawing to us the still-unsaved and permitting our Church to prevail as Jesus promised that she would. And not only prevail, but with the strength of the indwelling Holy Spirit do signs and wonders as occur only during times of great persecution. The times ahead will truly be exciting ones to the committed Christian, as Wisdom conversed with Earl in my novel *Cathy:*

"'So what's the mission?'

"'You're maturing as a Christian, so you've figured out by now that being a Christian isn't all fun and games.'

"Earl looked at Her with a growing concern, attempting to get from Her eyes a hint at what was coming next. 'I'm not sure that I like the sound of this. Where's it all heading?'

"'What do you think about the Rapture?'

"'We're ready. Joyce and I are really looking forward to it.'

"'Oh. So you think it's imminent.'

"'Well, yes I do. We do. Isn't it?' He said this last with a squeak of apprehension, which made Her laugh.

"'What's happening to my big Marine? Is that what you're waiting for? The Rapture for an easy out?'

"'Well - - kind of,' he admitted in a small voice.

"'Not going to happen. Not that way. You and a whole bunch of other very fine Christians have misled themselves and been misled by others with this misplaced hope. I'm afraid when the flag goes up you're going to be stuck right here in the thick of things, Earl. You and Joyce both. What do you say to that?'

"'Not much that I can say, is there? I'm disappointed, sure, but You're the boss. Not only that,' he said, reassembling his backbone, 'but I love You. All of You. Me and Joyce both. We'll do everything we can for Jesus' sake. With Your help, of course.'

"'Of course. I'll still be around, because you'll really be needing Me. Things are going to be heading south ever faster, and to many people it will seem like the Rapture actually happened. Chaos will become a normal state of affairs. Communications will be disrupted, and in the general turmoil it will seem like Christianity has departed from the face of the earth. To compound that general impression, many Christians are being persecuted as we speak. Many more will be following them, such that your ranks will be systematically decimated. Above and beyond that little item, a good many so-called Christians are falling away into open apostasy, further thinning out the ranks as they depart from the faith. But others – particularly Jews, beloved people of the Book, will get right with Us through their trials, and it'll be part of your job to help them get there.'"

Appendix One

Ten Reasons Why The Holy Spirit Must Be Of The Feminine Gender

The following reasons are taken from Scripture, and are consistent with a view of the Bible as inspired and inerrant in the original.

ONE: The original Old Testament Scripture in the Hebrew language described the Holy Spirit in feminine terms. Evidence of this has been furnished by several language-expert Bible scholars, among whom is R. P. Nettelhorst of the Quartz Hill School of Theology. Dr. Nettelhorst's specific examples include Genesis 1:2 that pointed to the role of the Holy Spirit in Creation and Judges 3:10, which represented a turning point in his understanding of God. He claims that there are 75 instances of either a feminine or indeterminable reference to the Holy Spirit, and no instances, other than descriptors of the Father, where in the original Hebrew the word "Spirit" is described in masculine terms. Other investigators have listed a multitude of specific Old Testament Bible passages that describe the Holy Spirit in feminine terms. Other passages, including Isaiah 51:9 and 10, furnish evidence of a deliberate switch of the Holy Spirit (Arm of the Lord) from feminine to masculine, as both feminine and masculine translations still exist, the feminine version being the earliest.

TWO: The original New Testament Scripture in the Greek/Aramaic language described the Holy Spirit in feminine terms, exposing a deliberate switch in descriptors from feminine to masculine. Evidence of this has been furnished by several Bible scholars, among whom is Johannes van Oort of Radboud University, Nijmegen, the

Netherlands, and the University of Pretoria, South Africa. Dr. van Oort, another language expert, claims that the primitive Christian Church, until at least through the second century A.D., and in some places through the fourth century A.D. spoke of the Holy Spirit as feminine. His sources include the Gospel of the Hebrews, which, while now lost, was quoted widely by early Christians, who noted that the Holy Spirit in that Gospel was described as feminine. He observed from the extensive quotations from that Gospel that it apparently was quite popular among the early Christians. Dr. van Oort notes that more modern Christian leaders, including John Wesley and Count von Zinzendorf of the Moravian Church, were influenced by quotes from that Gospel. Other investigators, including S. Santini and R. Nettelhorst, point to the Sinaitic Palimpsest, the earliest currently known of Gospel passages still extant, as quoting Jesus in John 14:26 as referencing the Holy Spirit in feminine terms. It is the originals that are to be respected for inspiration and accuracy, not the various translations. Next in line for respect, the earliest available versions are generally considered to be the most faithful to the original. Other passages, including Romans 9:25, retain an understanding of the Holy Spirit as feminine. It is important to note also that some of the interlinear translations of the Bible in Hebrew, Greek and Aramaic have also adjusted the language to conform to the Church tradition of replacing the feminine with the masculine.

   THREE: **The first Chapter of Genesis in commonly available translations and versions (including the King James) unequivocally depicts the Holy Spirit as feminine, regardless of the attempts to suppress that aspect of the Holy Spirit's nature.** The passage most strongly indicative of a feminine Holy Spirit is Genesis 1:26 and 27, which identifies the gendered nature of mankind as conforming to God's own nature. While modern commentators on this passage refuse to address this gender issue, they have no basis to do so other than participating in a slavish conformance to Church tradition, and are dishonest in their attempts to remove this characteristic from the image of God. Direct support of the depiction in Genesis 1 of the Holy Spirit's feminine nature is found in Psalm 94:9, wherein God describes attributes of man, specifically ears and eyes, asking why man can't understand that God possesses the same attributes. In that context, it would be appropriate for God to ask why, if man was made a gendered being, why God Himself wouldn't possess as well that same profoundly important attribute.

   FOUR: The account of the creation of Eve in Genesis 2 is a statement of the importance to God of gender. In opposition to the generally-accepted notion that the account of God's creation of Eve in Genesis 2 took place well after the creation of Adam as an incidental afterthought, the Genesis 2 account is so central to the intention of God that it is more detailed than the original description and is presented again for the purpose of emphasis. Back in Genesis 1:26-31, God already had created both Adam and Eve as gendered and capable of reproduction. Furthermore, it is in Genesis 1:31 that God describes His creation, including gendered humanity, as very good. In Genesis 2:18, God describes Adam without Eve as being not good, which would be a contradiction to the earlier account in Genesis 1 if Genesis 2 represented anything other than an emphatic revisit of Eve's creation. Yet more, in Matthew 19:4 and Mark 10:6-8, Jesus strongly defended the gendered nature of mankind as being the express intent of God from the beginning of Creation, pointing to its importance within the Godhead itself. This emphasis suggests the importance of Eve's creation from Adam to the extent that it says something about the gendered nature of the Godhead, which could easily be interpreted as a continuation of the information presented in Genesis 1:27 that the creation of Eve amounts to a reprise in mankind of God's own family nature.

FIVE: Only a union of a romantic, possessive nature between a male and a female is capable of fulfilling the passion intrinsic to God. Despite Church tradition that, influenced by the odd, cold theology of Zanchius and others of his cloth, the attributes of God include passion, and that passion includes romance. Scripture often attributes passion to Jesus and the other Members of the Godhead, most notably so in the Song of Solomon. The Song of Solomon is an overt description of gender-driven passion. Many respected Bible commentators see in this book a connection between Jesus and His Church in the spiritual domain, which places the attribute of gender firmly within the Godhead. Given the romantic, passionate nature of that Book, if romantic, possessive passion was not an attribute of God, the Song wouldn't belong in the canon of Scripture. Moreover, according to Jesus' greatest commandment to us in Matthew 22 (echoing Deuteronomy 6) God demands that same passion of us with respect to our relationship with Him. If God was incapable of experiencing that same passion, the commandment would be meaningless.

SIX: The selfless nobility intrinsic to God suggests a union within the Godhead of a harmony built upon complementary otherhood, which can only be fulfilled through gender differentiation. The Bible in its entirety, most emphatically presented in the work of Jesus on the cross, depicts God as selflessly noble. The alternatives to gender differentiation of an all-male or genderless Godhead would encourage narcissistic selfishness. The demand to love God with fervor requires us to view God in a family context as well. Any alternative to that view leaves us with confusion and a profound inability to obey the commandment of love that Jesus expressed in Matthew 22. The confusion is quite real: the confusion and lack of understanding has been confessed to me multiple times by theologians who possess impressive credentials, but who remain committed to a genderless or all-male Godhead. It is difficult to understand how a person who is confused about such an intimate detail regarding the nature of God would be able to worship Him with fervor.

SEVEN: In Ephesians 5, Paul claims that Jesus and His Church will be married, attributing functional gender to attributes within the Godhead. In Genesis 2, Adam states that Eve is bone of his bones and flesh of his flesh, and that therefore shall a man leave his father and his mother, and shall cleave unto his wife, and they shall be one flesh. The latter phrase represents the very words that Jesus repeated in Matthew 19:5 and 6, and in Mark 10:7 and 8. The importance of this phrase is confirmed in Ephesians 5:31 and 32, where Paul repeats it yet again, and then goes on to claim that it applies to the union of Jesus and His Church. Here, the Bible explicitly states that Jesus and the Church are fully gendered and will, in the spiritual domain, unite in marriage. That this union will be productive is asserted in Romans 7:4. The fact that Jesus is a Member of the Godhead and is slated to be married plainly suggests that the other two members of the Godhead are also gendered, and, in fact, are united with each other.

EIGHT: The Old Testament Shekinah Glory, generally **acknowledged to be feminine, is revealed in the New Testament as the Holy Spirit.** Paul goes to great lengths to describe the Church as a spiritual composite of individual Christians, in which the individuals are contributing elements of a whole, each individual being somewhat akin to the various organs that comprise a human body. In that context, gender is not important with regard to the individual (how would a gendered heart work?), but is a vital necessity, as in the complete human body, to the complete Church. An important aspect of the integrated spiritual Church is the indwelling Holy Spirit. As Paul declares in 1 Corinthians 3:16 and Ephesians 2:19-22, we Christians comprise a temple of God, wherein the Holy Spirit dwells. This temple described by Paul is a fulfillment of the type described in the Old Testament, where the Shekinah Glory indwelt the Tabernacle of the Wilderness and Solomon's Temple at their dedications (Exodus 40 and 1 Kings 8). The Shekinah Glory is generally acknowledged to be feminine in nature; the indwelling fulfillment in Christians identifies the Shekinah as the Holy Spirit.

NINE: The Book of Proverbs describes as feminine the Holy Spirit in Her role as complementary other to the Father. Proverbs 8:22-36, in particular, describes the Holy Spirit working alongside the Father in the Creation. That the feminine *Persona* of the Holy Spirit in Proverbs is far more than simply a figure of speech, is confirmed by Jesus Christ, who in Luke 7:35 described the Holy Spirit in terms of a sentient Mother. The connection between Wisdom and the Holy Spirit is also made in the Book of Wisdom, which, while having been removed from the canon of Protestant Scripture during the Reformation, remains canonical in the Catholic Church. In that book, Wisdom as a feminine Being is directly linked to the Holy Spirit.

TEN: In multiple passages, Jesus describes the Holy Spirit in feminine terms. In the Gospel of John, Jesus frequently links the Holy Spirit with feminine descriptors, such as "Comforter" and "Helper". This association is most direct in John 3, where Jesus connects the Holy Spirit with spiritual birth. Birth, of course, is an eminently feminine function. Moreover, many theologians see in Scripture the role of the Holy Spirit as an executive one. An executive function is feminine in nature, representing the essence of complementary otherhood in the carrying out of the will of the Father. More generally, even in translations that corrupt the original description of the Holy Spirit in feminine terms, the Holy Spirit in Genesis 1:2 is described as creatively responsive to the Father's will. A responsive role is a feminine one.

Appendix Two

Why Should It Matter?

The usual response to my multi-year heartfelt presentations of the Holy Spirit's femininity is glassy eyes and a shrug of the shoulders. *So what?* The body language says with eloquence. *Why should I care? Whoever or whatever God is or isn't, I'm a believer, so my faith is the only thing that really matters.*

But is it all that matters? More to the point, is faith without love really faith? In Matthew 22:37, Jesus echoes Moses' words in Deuteronomy 6:5 by claiming that the greatest commandment of God is that *Thou shalt love the Lord, thy God, with all thy heart, and with all thy soul, and with all thy mind.* Jesus stated that not as a suggestion, but as a commandment. Jesus also said in John 14:15 *If ye love me, keep my commandments.* These two passages can be paraphrased to say that your love must be fervent to truly be love.

Our faith itself must involve fervent love; otherwise, it isn't really faith at all, just some meaningless mind-exercise performed for the sake of acquiring peace of mind over the issue of where one goes after the game's up here on earth. But the faith of most of us is exactly that – fire insurance. Our worship of God seems to be based on a self-centered desire not to be left out of the joys of heaven (if heaven actually does exist, as we wonder within ourselves, and if it actually is joyful).

Fervent love toward God is far more than an exercise of the mind, because fervor doesn't come from the mind. It is an imprinting upon the soul akin to the passionate, possessive love between a man and a woman. It must be of such a magnitude that the thought of its removal invokes the same sense of desperate grief as the loss of a lifelong mate. It is the way that God made us to love Him. Anything less is not love, nor is it faith.

Less than fervent love has the potential of crumbling at the first threat to well-being. We see it happening now in the mass exodus from Church following the recent marginalization of Christians.

Here is where the issue of loving faith collides with our understanding of the nature of God. How can we possibly love that which we so imperfectly know? The Church for centuries has treated the Trinitarian Godhead as either void of gender or somewhat masculine, all three Members having essentially the same nature. The problem with that misrepresentation is that the Godhead and the functional roles within it are both alien and confusing. Some theologians, in recognizing that problem, have put forth the idea that each Member of the Godhead is endowed with traits belonging to both genders. But such theologians failed to use their heads: on a moral basis alone God's nobility resides far beyond such a narcissism-promoting arrangement as that would encourage. Beyond that issue, gender duality within each Member leaves unsolved the confusion of roles. Yet further, the gender ambiguity would attribute to God Himself gender traits which Scripture discourages in us. Because of the multiplicity of issues associated with it, most Churches recognize the problems inherent in that assignment, leaving us with the basic genderless or all-male model of the Godhead, returning us to confusion and alienation regarding the matter, which has led most Churches to ignore the issue completely.

But the issue is so important that it demands to be heard, for it involves faith. How can we worship God with the fervor He demands of us without even a basic understanding of who He is, and what little that we do know of Him is alien to us? That is exactly why the majority of self-styled Christians, lacking the love that God asks of us, are in blatant disobedience to God, holding to nothing more than a shallow semblance of faith. Most of us think more highly of ourselves than that, visualizing how we will hold fast to our faith in the face of persecution. But that kind of self-aggrandizing attitude is nothing but self-centered chest-pounding that will vaporize under any real threat.

The importance that I attach to this issue of the Holy Spirit's gender raises another issue of grave importance to all the millions of Christians who have lived and died over the many centuries that the Church has mischaracterized the Holy Spirit: has their failure to obey their God with the ardent love that He commanded denied them the eternal fellowship with God that He promised to His believers? Personally, I don't think that to be the case, particularly since the misleading came from the Church, not them. My belief that God is far more compassionate and merciful than that is reinforced by the numerous descriptions in Scripture of godly people who, at one time or another, failed to the extent of disobeying God's commandments. I certainly hope that He is that merciful, because I, for one, have been disobedient to God with distressing frequency.

Yet, if disobedience in loving God the way we should doesn't forever prohibit us from attaining favor with God, the issue of the Holy Spirit's feminine gender remains important to us regarding the depth of our commitment to God and to the advantages that are conferred upon us in the here and now for that understanding. For it is a great blessing to fellowship with God, and the closer we come to Him, the nearer that He comes and displays His love toward us. Then, of course, there is the matter of a shallow faith being subject to abandonment in the face of trouble, which is an issue that is not a threat to those closer to God.

In an enormous contrast to the prevailing state of affairs with the Church's misconception of God, an appreciation of a feminine Holy Spirit introduces the archetype of family into an understanding of the Godhead, instantly clarifying the respective roles of the individual Members and immediately removing all sense of confusion regarding the nature of God.

Most importantly, God is no longer alien to us, but One with whom we can identify through the personal experience of life itself. We can know this God intimately, and this intimacy grants us access to the kind of love that produces real faith in obedience to Jesus' command, a faith that is capable of withstanding all the negatives that life as Christians can bring us.

Principally because of the issue of holding fast to our faith under the pressure of worldly pleasures and the threat of persecution, the understanding of the Holy Spirit as of the feminine gender does indeed matter – under certain situations, it can be as important as the destination of our eternal souls.

There's still another reason for appreciating the Holy Spirit's feminine gender. Equipped with that understanding, a reading of Genesis 1 and 2 becomes a breathtakingly beautiful endeavor. For in the reading the prospect becomes convincing that these passages speak not only of the creation of mankind, but of the arrangement and roles within the Godhead itself of the Members comprising it. Is it not possible, then, that the Holy Spirit Herself was formed out of the Father's side in His effort to place Love above all other attributes of God, irretrievably far beyond self?

APPENDIX THREE

The First Light Of Creation

In Revelation 3:14, the risen Jesus delivers to John an admonishment regarding the seventh Church of His concern, the Church of Laodicea. In His description of that Church, He bypasses His usual format by omitting any mention of commendation. Of the seven Churches over which Jesus prophesied, only Sardis and Laodicea received that implicit chastisement. The Church of Laodicea, in fact is often cited by scholars of the Bible as representative of the fallen state of the Church at the time of the end of the age.

Focused on the characteristics of the Laodicean Church, scholars typically overlook the nature of the label that Jesus applied to Himself, which is odd because that statement contradicts the traditional doctrine of the mainstream Christian Church in a very important area.

> *"And unto the angel of the church of the Laodiceans write: These things saith the Amen, the faithful and true witness, the beginning of the creation of God."*

According to the Athanasian Creed and implicit in the others, including the Nicean Creed, Jesus had no beginning in time. The Father, the Son and the Holy Spirit were supposedly co-existent throughout eternity, none having been created. While in one sense that may be true, if one considers the pre-existence of one to include presence within another Being, that is not the usual interpretation of the creed as understood by the mainstream Churches, both Catholic and Protestant: Jesus and the Holy Spirit existed forever as separate Entities alongside the Father.

Yet there in Revelation 3:14 Jesus directly claims the opposite. If one must choose between a creed, which itself is extra-Scriptural, and Jesus, the very embodiment of truth, the obvious choice is Jesus.

The understanding that Jesus was created carries with it some very important collateral implications. In opposition to the mainstream Church's insistence upon God being genderless, which itself implies that procreation is a non-existent feature of the heavenly realm, this contradictory understanding solidifies the notion of the Holy Spirit's femininity, which, in turn, supports the characterization of the Holy Trinity as the embodiment of Family, complete with the function of procreation. The procreated Entity, in that context, is none other than Jesus Christ, the Son of the Father and of the Holy Spirit.

This identification clarifies a functional issue: Do the members of the Holy Trinity have the same or different functions, and if they are different, what are they? In the family context, with procreation on the table, the functions are indeed different, much as in an earthly family. Scripture itself identifies the Holy Father as embodying the divine Will. Scripture in John 6:38-40 exemplifies this association:

> "For I came down from heaven, not to do mine own will but the will of him who sent me. And this is the Father's will who hath sent me, that of all that he hath given me, I should lose nothing, but should raise iut up again at the last day. And this is the will of him who sent me, that everyone who seeth the Son, and believeth on him, may have everlasting life; and I will raise him up at the last day."

As divine spouse of the Father within the divine Family, the Holy Spirit must not only be feminine must embody a function that represents the perfect complement in the procreative sense. That would necessarily define the functional attribute of the Holy Spirit as one which would enable the implementation of the Father's will. A word for this enabling function would be "means". Thus the divine will, in union with the divine means, creates the Holy Son, the divine actuality Jesus Christ. It is Jesus, the divine implementation resulting from the union of will and means, who came into the created universe and represents the actuality of creation. John's Prologue, verses one through eighteen of John 1, says nothing less:

> "In the beginning was the Word, and the Word was with God, and the Word was God. The same was in the beginning with God. All things were made by him; and without him was not anything made

that was made. In him was life; and the life was the light of men. And the light shineth in darkness; and the darkness comprehended it not.

"There was a man sent from God, whose name was John. The same came for a witness, to bear witness of the Light, that all men though him might believe. He was not that Light, but was sent to bear witness to that Light.

"That was the true Light, which lighteth every man that cometh into the world. He was in the world, and the world was made by him, and the world knew him not. He came unto his own, and his own received him not. But as many as received him, to them gave he power to become the children of God, even to them that believe on his name; who were born, not of blood, nor of the will of the flesh, nor of the will of man, but of God. And the Word was made flesh, and dwelt among us (and we beheld his glory, the glory as of the only begotten of the Father), full of grace and truth.

"John bore witness of him, and cried, saying, This was he of whom I spoke, He that cometh after me is preferred before me; for he was before me. And of his fullness have all we received, and grace for grace. For the law was given by Moses, but grace and truth came by Jesus Christ.

"No man hath seen God at any time; the only begotten Son, who is in the bosom of the Father, he hath declared him."

In addition to declaring Him to be the actuality of creation, John's Prologue equates Jesus to both the Word and the Light. Given the nature of Jesus in this passage that is so fundamental to creation itself, Is there a context within the creation epic of Genesis in which Jesus is both the Word and the Light? The account in Genesis 1:14-19 that the sun and moon were created on the fourth day of creation places these bodies as having been created later than other events; futher, it doesn't implicate Jesus as the Word and the Light. But an earlier passage does, that of Genesis 1:3-5, and it is the first act of creation, following references to God and the Spirit working together:

"And God said, Let there be light; and there was light. And God saw the light, that it was good: and God divided the light from the darkness. And God called the light Day, and the darkness he called Night. And the evening and the morning were the first day."

In this passage God speaks. His first Word is the will for Light. We can assume from this that the Holy Spirit responded with the birth of the Light, the implementation of the Word of God – Jesus Christ, who acknowledged His birth in Revelation 3:14.

Is the Holy Spirit associated with birth elsewhere in Scripture? Yes, and directly indeed, from John 3:3-8:

> *"Jesus answered, and said unto [Nicodemus], Verily, verily, I say unto thee, Except a man be born again, he cannot see the kingdom of God. Nicodemus saith unto him, How can a man be born when he is old? Can he enter the second time unto his mother's womb, and be born? Jesus answered, Verily, verily, I say unto thee, Except a man be born of water and of the Spirit, he cannot enter into the kingdom of God. That which is born of the flesh is flesh; and that which is born of the Spirit is spirit. Marvel not that I said unto thee, Ye must be born again. The wind bloweth where it willeth, and thou hearest the sound of it, but canst not tell from where it cometh, and where it goeth; so is every one that is born of the Spirit."*

Given the obvious nature of birth as a feminine function, Jesus here directly identifies the Holy Spirit as feminine. Proverbs 8:22-31 is a more detailed and beautifully intimate narrative, delivered from the perspective of a feminine source, of the Holy Spirit's function as complementary to the Father's:

> *"The Lord possessed me in the beginning of his way, before his works of old. I was set up from everlasting, from the beginning, or ever the earth was. When there were no depths, I was brought forth – when there were no fountains abounding with water. Before the mountains were settled, before the hills, was I brought forth; while as yet he had not made the earth, nor the fields, nor the highest part of the dust of the world. When he prepared the heavens, I was there; when he set a compass upon the face of the depth; when he established the clouds above; when he strengthened the fountains of the deep; when he gave to the sea its decree, that the waters should not pass his commandment; when he appointed the foundations of the earth.*

> *"Then I was by him, as one brought up with him; and I was daily his delight, rejoicing always before him, rejoicing in the habitable part of his earth; and my delight was with the sons of men."*